Other books by Laurie Blum:

FREE MONEY FOR DAY CARE

FREE MONEY FOR FOREIGN STUDY

FREE MONEY FOR GRADUATE STUDY

FREE MONEY FOR HUMANITIES STUDENTS

FREE MONEY FOR HUMANITIES & SOCIAL SCIENCES

FREE MONEY FOR MATHEMATICS & NATURAL SCIENCES

FREE MONEY FOR PEOPLE IN THE ARTS

FREE MONEY FOR PRIVATE SCHOOLS

FREE MONEY FOR PROFESSIONAL STUDIES

FREE MONEY FOR SCIENCE STUDENTS

FREE MONEY FOR SMALL BUSINESSES & ENTREPRENEURS

FREE MONEY FOR UNDERGRADUATE STUDY

HOW TO GET FEDERAL GRANTS

HOW TO INVEST IN REAL ESTATE USING FREE MONEY

Laurie Blum's

FREE MONEY

for Heart Disease and Cancer Care

A Fireside Book
Published by Simon & Schuster
New York London Toronto Sydney Tokyo Singapore

F

FIRESIDE
Simon & Schuster Building
Rockefeller Center
1230 Avenue of the Americas
New York, New York 10020

FIRESIDE and colophon are registered trademarks
of Simon & Schuster Inc.

Designed by Christina M. Riley
Manufactured in the United States of America

1 3 5 7 9 10 8 6 4 2

Library of Congress Cataloging-in-Publication Data
is available

ISBN 0-671-74593-X

· · · · · · · · · · · · · · · · · · ·

I would like to briefly but sincerely thank my "A Team," Christina Riley, Deborah Brody, Tony Stanford, and Fori Kay, as well as my wonderful editor Ed Walters, and of course Alan Kellock.

Contents

· · · · · · · · · · · · · · · · · · ·

Foreword

by Harvey D'Zodin
Vice President, Cap Cities/ABC

The nation's health care system is in crisis. It is a hodge-podge of different groups (i.e., doctors, nurses, hospitals, government agencies, HMOs, and private insurers) laboring under a bewildering array of regulations and pursuing often contradictory objectives. No one is in charge. Power is fragmented.

It is little wonder that health care costs are going through the budgetary roof. Americans spent $600 billion on health care in 1989, double the national allocation for defense, and about 50% more than that spent for education. This is more than 11% of GNP (up from 9% in 1980). At the present rate of growth, the United States will spend $1.5 trillion by the year 2000! And, since 1980, employer-paid health insurance costs have risen three times faster than wages. Many businesses spend almost as much on health care as they earn in after-tax profits.

Good health care costs money. For those individuals who are afflicted with cancer or heart disease, the good news is that cancer and heart disease are among the most curable of chronic illnesses. The bad news, however, is that failure to locate the best, most advanced care available can mean the difference between life and death. Some 38 million people have no health insurance. Those who are insured still pay a portion of routine medical expenses because of deductible and coinsurance provisions. Many are not protected financially from catastrophic illness, or have only partial protection from the high costs of various kinds of serious illness. Sixty million Americans below the age of 65 face unlimited out-of-pocket expenses in the event of catastrophic illness. Laurie Blum's timely book gives you a wealth of financial information and resources to help you bear the costs associated with heart disease and cancer.

I am very proud of my good friend Laurie Blum for writing this much-needed book. While I wish that this book had existed during my wife's unfortunately unsuccessful battle with cancer, there is great satisfaction in knowing that it will help many cancer and heart disease patients become survivors.

Introduction

In 1989, the total cost of American health care was $600 billion — twice what the Pentagon spent, and half again as much as the country's total outlay for education. Health care currently accounts for 11% of the gross national product, up from 9% in 1980, and is expected to rise to 13% during the present decade. It surprises no one that medical costs have increased — and continue to increase — at a rate faster than the growth of the overall economy and higher than the rate of inflation.

What does surprise many is the extent to which American consumers pay directly for their own medical care: total out-of-pocket costs reached $175 billion last year. Private insurers covered another $186 billion, and the balance of $239 billion was paid by the three M's of federal government health care: Medicare, Medicaid and the Military.

American consumers pay directly for 29% of the nation's total medical costs for a number of reasons. Some 38 million people have no health insurance. Those who are insured still pay a portion of routine medical expenses because of deductible and coinsurance provisions. Even with insurance, many are not protected financially from catastrophic illness, or have only partial protection from the high costs of various kinds of serious illness. Sixty million Americans below the age of 65 face unlimited out-of-pocket expenses in the event of catastrophic illness.

Free Money for Heart Disease and Cancer Care directs readers to the billions of dollars available annually to provide both aid for direct medical expenses (such as doctor and hospital bills) and reimbursement for the loss of regular income, which is often a devastating side-effect of illness. Much of the available money is awarded without regard to the financial status of the recipient, and *none* of it ever needs to be paid back. The book includes information on funding available in all fifty states.

The book is divided into six chapters:

1) **"Associations: Funding and Referral Information"** (listing heart and cancer foundations and associations that provide a wide range of services, including: supplying information on the disease; sponsoring and referring patients and their families to support groups; and providing physician referrals, funds for research, and patient services);

2) **"Private Foundation Funding"** (listing possible sources both for monies for direct medical expenses such as doctor and hospital bills, and for reimbursement for the loss of regular income that is often a devastating side-effect of illness);

3) **"Corporate/Employee Grants"** (listing companies and corporations that provide grants for their employees or former employees);

4) **"Flow-through Funding"** (providing information about foundation monies that are given to individuals through sponsoring nonprofit organizations);

5) **"State and Regional Government Grants"** (including local state health care offices, as well as native health service grants, which provide funds for American Indians and Native Alaskans); and

6) **"Federal Grants"** (identifying agencies offering direct funding and/or essential referral information).

Where possible, listings within each chapter are arranged state-by-state to make this book as easy to use as possible. Check your state's listings in all six chapters to see which grants or corporate programs apply to you. You'll find funding parameters and an address and phone number to contact for further information (and application forms).

By the time this book is published, some of the information contained here will have changed. No reference book can be as up-to-date as the reader or the author would like.

Names, addresses, dollar amounts, telephone numbers, and other data are always in flux; however, most of the information will not have changed.

While reviewing this data, readers are advised to remember that funding sources are not without restrictions and that researching, applying for, and receiving aid will take time, effort, diligence, and thought. You are going to have to identify the sources of aid for which you qualify and determine whether or not you fulfill geographic and other requirements. You are going to have to fill out applications. You may meet with rejection and frustration somewhere along this road. The odds, however, are in your favor that you will qualify for some sort of funding assistance.

On the next pages is a concise, how-to guide to writing a grant proposal. Follow my instructions and you should be successful in obtaining some sort of assistance. Good luck.

How to apply

．．．．．．．．．．．．．．．．．．．

As indicated by the number of listings in this book,
thousands of resources for health-related funding exist
throughout the country from government, private foundation, and corporate sources. Applying for this aid is the
challenging part; it requires diligence, thought and
organization.

First is the sorting out or research/gathering phase. Look through
each chapter of the book and mark each potential assistance source. Pay close attention to the listed restrictions
and qualifications, eliminating from your list the resources
least likely to assist you.

Then, politely contact each of your listed sources by mail or
phone to verify all current information, such as address,
telephone, name of the proper contact, and his/her title (in
cases where the contact's name is not listed, begin your
letter, "To Whom It May Concern"). At this time, you can
also arrange to get a copy of the source's most current
assistance guidelines, and an application form if one is
required. Use this opportunity to find out about any
application deadlines and to ask where you are in the
funding cycle (i.e., if there is no deadline, when would be
the best time to apply; also, be sure to ask when awards
will be announced and funds distributed). However, do not
"grill" or cross-examine the person you reach on the phone.
Always be prepared to talk about why you are applying and
what you are applying for — in case you ring through to
the key decisionmaker, who decides to interview you on the
spot!

Second is the application phase. Most often you will be asked to submit a formal application (rather than a proposal). Always be sure to read (and follow!) the instructions for completing the application. Usually the same material used for one application can be applied to most, if not all, of your other applications, with a little restructuring to make sure you answer each and every question as asked, appropriate to each application.

Grant applications take time (and thought) to fill out, so make sure you give yourself enough time to thoroughly complete the application before its deadline. Filling out the application can be a lengthy process, because you may be required to write one or more essays. Often, what is required is a "statement of purpose" explaining what you will use the money for and sometimes explaining why you need the assistance for which you are applying. You may also need time to assemble required attachments, such as tax returns and other financial records. (Don't worry, in most cases, you won't be penalized for having money in the bank.) You may also be required to include personal references. Be sure to get strong references. Call all of the people you plan to list, and ask them if they feel comfortable giving you references. Remember, you have to convince the grantors to give money to you and not to someone else.

Be clear, concise and neat! You may very well prepare a top-notch application, but it won't look good if it's been prepared in a sloppy manner. Applications (and proposals) should always be typed and double-spaced. Make sure you keep a copy after you send off the original — I have learned the hard way that there is nothing worse than having the funding source be unable to find your application and your having to reconstruct it because you didn't keep a copy.

You should apply to a number of funding sources for grants and awards, as no one application is guaranteed to win an award. Although none of the sources listed in this book requires an application fee, the effort you will have to put in will probably limit you to a maximum of eight applications (if you are ambitious and want to apply to more than eight sources, go right ahead). Remember, the more sources you apply to, the greater your chances for success.

COMPONENTS OF
A SUCCESSFUL PROPOSAL

One of the largest categories of grants that are given to individuals are grants for general welfare and medical assistance, that is "free money" for emergency or long-term personal, medical, or living expenses. The various funding agencies that make these awards have happily made applying for these grants much simpler than for other categories. Most, if not all, of the foundations you will be applying to will require the following in order to consider your request for funding:

1. A brief but concise letter outlining you or your family member's medical problem and/or expenses and bills you have incurred because of this problem. In the final paragraph of your letter you should specify a dollar amount that you feel confident would ease your financial burden (i.e., "I request a grant in the amount of $2,500 to help me pay the costs associated with a visiting nurse which is not covered by my medical insurance."). Remember to carefully look at the money given in the foundation listing you are applying to; If the foundation only gives grants ranging from $5,000 to $15,000 and you need $20,000, you can only request that which the foundation gives.

2. A report from the doctors or hospital staff involved with the patient on whose behalf the grant is being submitted. Because of the enormous volume of mail that most foundations receive, you may want to get the medical reports directly from doctors and/or hospital personnel and submit them with your application. This way there is no chance that a foundation can delay or turn down your application on the grounds that it is incomplete.

3. A copy of your tax return. Do not panic! You will not be penalized for showing excellent earnings or having savings. The issue is how the costs associated with the medical problems or care needs that you are faced with alter your financial stability. However, if you are in financial need you will certainly be given every consideration.

4. A personal interview. This may take place by phone or in person. Stay calm. Foundations are run by people committed to their mission of helping those in need or in trouble. Simply state the facts of your case and needs and all will go well.

Remember, your application should be clear and concise. Your letter should not exceed two pages. Be sure to include any attachments the foundation might require such as medical reports and tax returns. Follow my instructions and you should qualify for some sort of "free money."

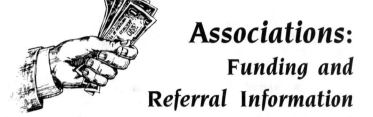

Associations:
Funding and
Referral Information

· · · · · · · · · · · · · · · · · · · ·

This chapter is an invaluable resource guide for the patient and his/her family. It contains listings of foundations/associations that address the needs of individuals with specific diseases. Among the many services they provide, these organizations publish information about the disease, sponsor and refer patients and their families to support groups, give physician referrals, and award funds for research as well as for patient services. Though not all of the foundations/associations offer monies to be paid directly to patients, I felt it was imperative that I include this information in this book. Having experienced catastrophic illness firsthand, I know all too well the comfort and support that a professional association offers the patient and his/her family, who are frightened and overwhelmed.

The chapter is organized alphabetically, by name of disease. The various associations/foundations are listed alphabetically under the names of the diseases they address.

Patients and their families will probably find, as I have, that the various staff members of these foundations/associations are exceedingly helpful during difficult times. Use them and their associations to your best advantage.

ASSOCIATIONS

. . . .

ASSOCIATIONS FOR HEART DISEASES

American Association of Cardiovascular and Pulmonary Rehabilitation
7611 Elmwood Avenue
Suite 201
Middleton, WI 53562
(608) 831-6989

Description: Allied health professionals involved in the field of cardiovascular and pulmonary rehabilitation; fosters the improvement of clinical practice in CVPR; promotes scientific CVPR research; seeks the advancement of CVPR education for health care professionals and the public
Contact: Jane C. Shepard, Executive Director

American College of Cardiology
9111 Old Georgetown Road
Bethseda, MD 20814
(301) 897-5400

Description: Professional society of physicians, surgeons, and scientists specializing in cardiology (heart) and cardiovascular (circulatory) diseases; operates Heart House Learning Center, and a library of 1,500 volumes
Contact: William D. Nelligan, CAE, Executive Vice President

Association of Black Cardiologists
2300 Garrison Blvd.
Suite 150
Baltimore, MD 21216
(301) 945-2525

Description: Seeks to improve prevention and treatment of cardiovascular diseases; conducts educational and research programs; bestows awards; maintains speakers' bureau
Contact: B. Waine Kong, Ph.D., Executive Director

American Heart Association
7320 Greenville Avenue
Dallas, TX 75231
(214) 373-6300

Description: Physicians, scientists, and laypersons who support research, education, and community service programs with the objective of reducing premature deaths and disability from cardiovascular disease and strokes
Contact: Dudley F. Hafner, Executive Vice President

Coronary Club
9500 Euclid Avenue
Cleveland, OH 44106
(216) 444-3690

Description: Heart patients, doctors, nurses, therapists, educators and other health professionals involved in cardiac care; seeks to provide members with information on all facets of heart care via a bulletin written by a cardiologist in lay language
Contact: Kathryn E. Ryan, Administrative Assistant

Heart Disease Research Foundation
50 Court Street
Brooklyn, NY 11201
(718) 649-6210

Description: Promotes research aimed at the prevention, early diagnosis, and treatment of cardiovascular disease and related medico-social problems; conducts public education programs on the heart and heart disease; answers questions from the public and professionals
Contact: Dr. Yoshiaki Omura, Medical Research Director

Mended Hearts
7320 Greenville Avenue
Dallas, TX 75231
(214) 706-1442

Description: Provides advice, encouragement, and services to heart disease patients, their families, and friends.
Contact: Darla Bonham, Executive Director

National Heart Savers Association
4601 S. 76th Street
Omaha, NE 68127
(402) 339-3813

Description: Promotes cardiac health by informing the public of the dangers of a high fat and cholesterol diet; conducts public health cholesterol screenings
Contact: Phil Sokolof, President

ASSOCIATIONS

. . . .

ASSOCIATIONS FOR CANCER AND CANCER RELATED DISORDERS

American Cancer Society
1559 Clifton Road, NE
Atlanta, GA 30329
(404) 320-3333
(800) ACS-2345

Description: Promotes education and research in cancer prevention, diagnosis, detection and treatment; offers special services to cancer patients
Contact: William M. Tipping, Executive Vice President

Association for Brain Tumor Research (Cancer)
3725 N. Talman Avenue
Chicago, IL 60618
(312) 286-5571

Description: Objective is to raise funds for brain tumor research, distribute patient education information on brain tumors and brain tumor research, and to increase public awareness; provides referral service
Contact: Naomi Berkowitz, Executive Director

Association for Research of Childhood Cancer
P.O. Box 251
Buffalo, NY 14225
(716) 681-4433

Description: Funds the expansion and continuation of research in pediatric cancer centers and provides seed money for pilot projects in cancer research; provides support to parents of children with cancer
Contact: Charles Moll, Executive Officer

Breast Cancer Advisory Center
P.O. Box 224
Kensington, MD 20895
FAX (301) 949-1132

Description: A medical service group for people with breast cancer; makes referrals, distributes information, and gives lectures
Contact: Rose Kusher, Executive Director

• • • • • • • • • • • • • • • • • • •

Cancer Federation, Inc.
21250 Box Springs Road
No. 209
Moreno Valley, CA 92387
(714) 682-7989

Description: Supports research and education in the field of cancer immunology; provides counseling programs for cancer patients and their families
Contact: John Steinbacher, Executive Director

Cancer Guidance Institute
1323 Forbes Avenue
Suite 200
Pittsburgh, PA 15219
(412) 261-2211

Description: Goal is to help patients cope with the psychological impact of cancer; stresses the importance of the patients's attitude and emotions in the recovery process; encourages patients to aid each other with both the practical and psychological aspects of the healing process; provides consulting services.
Contact: Estelle Weissburg, Executive Director

Cancer Information Services
Boy Scout Building
Room 340
9000 Rockville Pike
Bethseda, MD 20892
(301) 496-8664
(800) 4-CANCER hotline

Description: Counselors provide information about cancer causes, prevention, detection, diagnosis, rehabilitation, and research; distributes a variety of publications on cancer to patients and their families
Contact: Kate Duffy, Executive Officer

Candlelighters Childhood Cancer Foundation
1312 18th Street NW
No. 200
Washington, DC 20036
(202) 659-5136

Description: Offers guidance and emotional support for families of children with cancer and identifies patient and family needs to enable medical and social systems to respond adequately; provides 24-hour crisis lines, babysitting, and transportation services; sponsors blood and wig banks, immune programs, and the establishment of Ronald McDonald residences for families of children requiring extended care away from home
Contact: Julie Sullivan, Executive Director

ASSOCIATIONS

Corporate Angel Network
Westchester County Airport
Building One
White Plains, NY 10604
(914) 328-1313

Description: An association of United States corporate aircraft owners who offer empty seats to cancer patients in need of transportation to or from recognized treatment centers; patients must be able to board the aircraft unassisted, must not require special equipment or services en route, and must have proper medical authorization for the flight; C.A.N. will also transport one attendant or family member with the patient (patient must provide his or her own ground transportation)
Contact: Judith Haims, Administrator

Gynecologic Oncology Group
1234 Market Street
No. 1945
Philadelphia, PA 19107
(215) 854-0770

Description: Composed of institutions and teaching hospitals conducting research in gynecological oncology
Contact: John R. Kellner, Manager

International Health Council (Cancer)
P.O. Box 151
Fairbanks, AK 99707

Description: Organization of medical professionals and lay volunteers devoted to the prevention of cancer deaths; promotes early detection and treatment by making people aware of early symptoms and proper treatment programs
Contact: Walter Ermer, Executive Director

Komen Foundation (Cancer)
6820 LBJ Freeway
Suite 130
Dallas, TX 75240
(214) 980-8841
(800) IM-AWARE

Description: Strives to increase the recovery and survival rates of breast cancer patients and to heighten public awareness of the risks of breast cancer and the need for early detection; funds research and treatment programs
Contact: Linda R. Cadigan, Executive Director

• • • • • • • • • • • • • • • • • •

Leukemia Society of America
733 Third Avenue
New York, NY 10017
(212) 573-8484

Description: Combats leukemia by funding research, patient services, and public and professional education; offers financial aid to patients and sponsors support groups
Contact: Peter N. Cakrides, President

Make Today Count
101 1/2 South Union Street
Alexandria, VA 22314
(703) 548-9674

Description: Brings cancer patients and their families and neighbors together to discuss openly the false implications and the realities of life-threatening diseases; stresses a positive approach to the problems of serious illness in order to lessen the emotional trauma for all concerned; helps professionals to communicate with and meet the needs of seriously ill patients
Contact: Sandra Butler Whyte, Executive Director

National Alliance of Breast Cancer Organizations
1180 Avenue of the Americas
Second Floor
New York, NY 10036
(212) 719-0154

Description: Acts as a resource for individuals seeking information about research, developments and treatment options for breast cancer; distributes educational materials and information on support groups, breast care centers, and various hospital programs
Contact: Amy Langer, Administrative Director

National Cancer Center
88 Sunnyside Blvd.
Plainview, NY 11803
(516) 349-0610

Description: Provides support for cancer research and educational programs.
Contact: Regina English, Executive Director

National Coalition for Cancer Survivorship
106 8th Street SW
Albuquerque, NM 87102
(505) 764-9956

Description: Distributes information on supporting and helping survivors deal with life after a cancer diagnosis
Contact: Catherine Logan, Executive Director

ASSOCIATIONS

. . . .

National Leukemia Association
585 Stewart Avenue
Suite 536
Garden City, NY 11530
(516) 222-1944

Description: Promotes leukemia research and public awareness of the disease, and provides financial aid to leukemia patients and their families (based on need)
Contact: Allan D. Weinberg, Executive Director

R.A. Bloch Cancer Foundation
H and R Block Building
4410 Main Street
Kansas City, MO 64111
(816) 932-8453

Description: Primary service is the Cancer Hot Line, a support group that matches cancer patients with volunteers who have been cured, are in remission, or are being treated for the same type of cancer; volunteers describe the treatments they have received and offer information referrals to newly-diagnosed cancer victims; Cancer Hot Lines operate in St. Louis and Kansas City, Missouri; Ft. Lauderdale, Florida; Ft. Worth, Texas; Oklahoma City, Oklahoma; Cleveland, Ohio; and Pittsburgh, Pennsylvania; volunteers also conduct long-distance counseling by telephone
Contact: Wanda L. Chernoff, Executive Director

Reach to Recovery
c/o American Cancer Society
1599 Cliffton Road NE
Atlanta, GA 30329
(404) 320-3333

Description: A peer visitor program for women who have or have had breast cancer; strives to help women meet the physical, emotional, and cosmetic needs related to their disease and its treatment
Contact: Claudia Bannon

Spirit and Breath Association
8210 Elmwood Avenue
Suite 209
Skokie, IL 60077
(708) 673-1384

Description: Provides a forum for discussion and an information exchange for individuals who are undergoing or have undergone treatment for lung cancer
Contact: Morton Leibling, Founder and Director

• •

United Cancer Council
4010 West 86th Street
Suite H
Indianapolis, IN 46268

Description: Association of independent cancer agencies who receive their support from the United Way of America, which promotes programs of direct service to cancer patients and encourages public and professional education regarding the cause and cure of cancer
Contact: Randall B. Grove, President

We Can Do!
c/o Jackalyn Rainosek
1800 Augusta
Suite 150
Houston, TX 77057
(713) 780-1057

Description: Association of cancer patients and professional psychologists whose objective is to serve as a support system for patients and their families; offers therapy program for patients using methods of stress reduction, relaxation, guided imagery, and biofeedback
Contact: Jackalyn Rainosek, Executive Officer

Y-ME National Organization for Breast Cancer Information and Support
c/o Sharon Green
18220 Harwood Avenue
Homewood, IL 60430
(708) 799-8338

Description: Provides peer support and information to women who have or suspect they have breast cancer; activities include pre-surgical counseling and referral service, inservice programs for health professionals, hot line volunteer training, and technical assistance
Contact: Sharon Green, Executive Director

Private Foundation Funding

The listings in this chapter are probably the easiest and most accessible funding sources for the average individual seeking a grant. Until now, this information has not been readily available to the general public. And yet thousands of foundations give away millions of dollars to individuals to help them pay for medical treatment for major, long-term and chronic illnesses. In many cases, foundations also provide funding to help individuals cope with the loss of regular income that is often a devastating side-effect of such illnesses.

Do you just walk up, hold out your hand, and expect someone to put money in it? Of course not. Getting grant money takes time, effort, and thought on your part. You are going to have to find out who is giving away money. You are going to have to fill out applications. You may meet with frustration or rejection somewhere down the road. The odds, however, are in your favor that you will qualify for some sort of funding.

The information in this chapter is organized by state. Wherever possible, each listing includes a description of what the foundation funds, any restrictions (i.e., you must reside in a particular town or city), the total amount of money awarded annually, the number of grants or loans made annually, the range of monies given, the average size of the award, information on how to apply, deadline date(s), and name(s) of contact person(s).

PRIVATE FOUNDATION FUNDING

. . . .

ALABAMA

Kate Kinloch Middleton Fund
P.O. Drawer 2527
Mobile, AL 36601
phone: N/A

Description: Grants or low interest loans to help defray the costs of unexpected serious illness
Restrictions: Limited to residents of Mobile County, Alabama
$ Given: In FY89, 63 grants totaling $108,286 were awarded to individuals; range, $135 - $8,094.
Application Information: Initial approach by interview
Deadline: N/A
Contact: Joan Sapp

CALIFORNIA

William Babcock Memorial Endowment
305 San Anselmo Avenue
Suite 219
San Anselmo, CA 94960
(415) 453-0901

Description: Grants Grants and loans to persons burdened with exceptional medical expenses which exceed insurance coverage and fall outside the purview of other community agencies
Restrictions: Limited to persons who have been residents of Marin County, California, for two or more years
$ Given: In FY89, 480 grants totaling $445,170 were awarded to individuals; range, $50 - $10,000.
Application Information: Call for application guidelines; formal application required
Deadline: None
Contact: Executive Director

Albert B. Cutter Memorial Fund
Security Pacific National Bank
Trust Department
P.O. Box 712
Riverside, CA 92501
(714) 781-1523
ADDITIONAL ADDRESS:
P.O. Box 3189
Terminal Annex
Los Angeles, CA 92501

Description: Limited grants to persons in extreme circumstances who are not eligible for other sources of aid
Restrictions: Applicants must have been permanent residents of Riverside, California for at least one year, and must have been referred by a local agency
$ Given: In 1989, 26 grants totaling $6,650 were awarded to individuals; range, $22 - $550.
Application Information: Applications are accepted from local agencies; individuals are referred by these agencies; formal application required; interview or presentation required
Deadline: None
Contact: Executive Secretary, Trust Department

Jefferson (John Percival and Mary C.) Endowment Fund
114 East De La Guerra
Santa Barbara, CA 93102
(805) 963-8822

Description: Emergency relief assistance for medical, dental and living expenses
Restrictions: Limited to residents of Santa Barbara County, California
$ Given: In FY89, 30 grants totaling $63,000 were awarded to individuals; range, $100 - $6,500.
Application Information: Initial contact by letter; formal application required
Deadline: N/A
Contact: Patricia M. Brouard, Trustee

PRIVATE FOUNDATION FUNDING

• • • • • • • • • • • • • • • • • • • •

Charles E. Saak Trust
c/o Wells Fargo Bank
Trust Department
2222 West Shaw Avenue
Suite 11
Fresno, CA 93711
(209) 442-6232
(209) 442-6206

Description: One-time grants for dental and emergency medical assistance to children under 21 years of age from low-income families. Each award is designed to cover the total cost (up to the total grant award) of one injury, sickness or dental treatment. Unpredicted additional costs for the same treatment must be approved in advance by the trustee
Restrictions: Limited to residents of the Porterville/Poplar area of Tulare County, California
$ Given: In FY89, 140 grants totaling $42,380 were awarded to individuals; range, $51 - $1,375; general range, $300 - $900.
Application Information: Formal application required; include purpose and cost estimate statement, parents' financial statement (include a copy of most recent income tax return)
Deadline: March 31
Contact: N/A

Virginia Scatena Memorial Fund for San Francisco School Teachers
c/o Bank of America, N.A.
555 California Street
17th Floor
San Francisco, CA 94104
phone: N/A

Description: Financial assistance to retired San Francisco school teachers who are needy, sick or disabled
Restrictions: Limited to retired teachers of the San Francisco Public School Department
$ Given: Total grants range from $125 - $400.
Application Information: Formal application required
Deadline: None; applications reviewed semi-annually by advisory committee
Contact: Susan Morales

• • • • • • • • • • • • • • • • • • • •

Sequoia Trust Fund
555 California Street
36th Floor
San Francisco, CA 94104
(415) 393-8552

Description: Financial assistance "to needy people who, by their special talents, have given great pleasure to others"
Restrictions: Assistance for special or unusual medical expenses; primarily for California residents
$ Given: In FY89, two grants totaling $4,400 were awarded to individuals; range, $2,000 - $2,400.
Application Information: Initial contact by letter; formal application required
Deadline: None
Contact: Walter M. Baird, Secretary

COLORADO

Curtis (Effie H. and Edward H.) Trust Fund
c/o United Bank of Fort Collins, N.A.
P.O. Box 2203
Fort Collins, CO 80522
(303) 482-1100

Description: Grants for emergency medical assistance, paid directly to hospitals and other medical institutions to benefit grant recipients
Restrictions: Limited to permanent residents of Larimer County, Colorado who are under 18 years old.
$ Given: In 1989, 46 grants totaling $40,000 were awarded to individuals; range, $15 - $3,000
Application Information: Formal application required, including letter from attending physician; include copy of tax return
Deadline: 15th of each month
Contact: Kelly Wiedeman

PRIVATE FOUNDATION FUNDING

· · · · · · · · · · · · · · · · · · · ·

CONNECTICUT

**Blue Horizon Health &
Welfare Trust**
c/o Reid & Riege
Lakeville, CT 06039
(203) 435-9251

Description: Financial assistance for medical costs
Restrictions: Limited to residents of Connecticut
$ Given: Grant awards range from $25 - 500.
Application Information: Initial contact by letter
Deadline: None
Contact: Frances M. Wagner, Trustee

Marion Isabelle Coe Fund
c/o Colonial Bank and
Trust Company
P.O. Box 2210
Waterbury, CT 06722
phone: N/A

Description: Relief assistance to adults for general living
and medical expenses. Grants provide continuing
assistance to needy individuals to enable them to
remain in their own homes. Awards paid in monthly
installments, and are renewed annually
Restrictions: Limited to residents of Goshen, Litchfield,
Morris, and Warren, Connecticut
$ Given: Monthly awards range from $45 to $140;
average, $100
Application Information: Initial contact by letter
Deadline: None
Contact: Mrs. Speers

**James Crocker
Testamentary Trust**
P.O. Box 1045
Canaan, CT 06018
phone: N/A

Description: Temporary assistance to individuals in
extreme financial difficulty
Restrictions: Limited to residents of Winchester, Connecticut
$ Given: Grants range from $100 - 500.
Application Information: Most applications are
unsolicited and not preselected. Applicants are typically
referred to the Funds Manager by local clergy of all
denominations. Information concerning immediate
financial need required.
Deadline: N/A
Contact: Kevin F. Nelligan

● ● ● ● ● ● ● ● ● ● ● ● ● ● ● ● ● ●

The de Kay Foundation
c/o Manufacturers Hanover
Trust Company
270 Park Avenue
New York, NY 10017
(212) 270-6000

Description: Grants to elderly individuals in financial need, particularly to those who are sick or disabled or who lack proper care
Restrictions: Limited to residents of New York, New Jersey and Connecticut
$ Given: In FY89, 83 grants totaling $202,540 were awarded to individuals; range, $350 - $7,150; general range, $1,000 - $5, 000.
Application Information: Initial approach by letter; formal application required
Deadline: None
Contact: Lloyd Saltus II, Vice President

**St. Luke's Nurses
Benefit Fund**
47 Phillips Lane
Darien, CT 06820
phone: N/A

Description: Grants for needy graduates of St. Luke's School of Nursing
Restrictions: Limited to St. Luke's alumnae
$ Given: In FY89, one grant for $2,000 was awarded.
Application Information: Formal application required
Deadline: None
Contact: Martha Kirk, Trustee

**The Westport-Weston
Foundation**
c/o The Westport Bank &
Trust Company
P.O. Box 5177
Westport, CT 06881
(203) 222-6911

Description: Grants for medical and basic living expenses
Restrictions: Limited to residents of Westport and Weston, Connecticut
$ Given: Grants range from $50 - $400.
Application Information: Initial contact by letter
Deadline: N/A
Contact: Susanne M. Allen, Trust Officer

PRIVATE FOUNDATION FUNDING

Widow's Society
20 Bayberry Lane
Avon, CT 06001
(203) 678-9660

Description: Financial assistance to needy women
Restrictions: Limited to residents of Connecticut
$ Given: In FY89, 118 grants totaling $122,824 were awarded to individuals; range, $75 - $4,800.
Application Information: Applications are typically referred through social service agencies, but individuals may also submit letters
Deadline: N/A
Contact: Dorothy Johnson, President

DELAWARE

**Delaware Foundation -
Quigly Trust**
P.O. Box 1669
Wilmington, DE 19899
phone: N/A

Description: Grants for medication and medical care
Restrictions: Limited to residents of Delaware
$ Given: Grants range from $50 - $1,500.
Application Information: Formal application required; request application form from the foundation
Deadline: None
Contact: N/A

FLORIDA

**Gore Family Memorial
Foundation**
501 East Las Olas
Fort Lauderdale, FL 33302
phone: N/A

Description: One-time and short-term assistance grants for medical expenses, equipment for the handicapped, and housing and transportation costs
Restrictions: Limited to residents of Broward County, Florida, and surrounding areas
$ Given: In FY89, 390 relief assistance grants totaling $279,250 were awarded to individuals.
Application Information: Write for application guidelines
Deadline: None
Contact: N/A

• • • • • • • • • • • • • • • • • • • •

Roy M. Speer Foundation
1803 U.S. Highway 19
Holiday, FL 34691-5536
phone: N/A

Description: Grants to individuals in financial difficulty as a result of medical problems
Restrictions: Limited to residents of Florida
$ Given: One grant for $4,000 is awarded.
Application Information: Initial approach by letter
Deadline: None
Contact: N/A

Winter Haven Hospital Charity Fund
c/o NCNB National Bank
P.O. Box 199
Orlando, FL 32802
phone: N/A

Description: Grants for medical assistance for the financially distressed
Restrictions: Limited to residents of Winter Haven, Florida
$ Given: In FY89, two grants were awarded to individuals; range, $250 - $1,500.
Application Information: Write for guidelines
Deadline: None
Contact: N/A

GEORGIA

Baker (Clark and Ruby) Foundation
c/o Bank South
Personal Trust Department
P.O. Box 4956 (MC45)
Atlanta, GA 30302-9824
(404) 529-4627

Description: Grants primarily to retired Methodist ministers for pensions and medical assistance
Restrictions: Residents of Georgia
$ Given: 10 grants totaling $15,500 are awarded to individuals.
Application Information: Initial approach by letter or phone; interviews required
Deadline: None
Contact: Richard L. Watton, Trust Officer

PRIVATE FOUNDATION FUNDING

• • • • • • • • • • • • • • • • • • • •

Thomas C. Burke Foundation
182 Riley Avenue
No. B
Macon, GA 31204-2345
(912) 745-1442

Description: Medical assistance in one of three forms: (1) one-time payments for doctor bills, medical equipment and pharmacy bills; (2) weekly grants of up to $60 to assist with medical expenses; or (3) grants for transportation to medical facilities
Restrictions: Limited to residents of Bibb County, Georgia
$ Given: In FY89, an unspecified number of grants totaling $120,772 were awarded to individuals.
Application Information: Initial contact by phone
Deadline: None
Contact: Carolyn P. Griggers

Pine Mountain Benevolent Foundation, Inc.
P.O. Box 2301
Columbus, GA 31902
phone: N/A

Description: Welfare assistance to individuals living in Georgia
Restrictions: Limited to residents of Georgia
$ Given: In FY89, two grants totaling $2,200 were awarded to individuals; range, $500 - $1,500.
Application Information: Write for guidelines
Deadline: None
Contact: Cason J. Callaway, Jr.

HAWAII

The Hawaii Community Foundation
222 Merchant Street
Honolulu, HI 96813
(808) 537-6333

Program: Winifred D. Robertson Fund
Description: One-time assistance to adult residents of Oahu, Hawaii

Program: Alice M.G. Soper Fund
Description: One-time grants to adults, age 50 or older in financial need due to illness or disability

Program: Gwenfried Allen Fund
Description: Financial assistance for the elderly and mentally ill

Program: Irving L. Singer Funds
Description: One-time assistance to children of Hawaiian ancestry whose families are unable to pay for medical expenses, or for special education, social services, or mental health services

Program: The Kitaro Watanabe Fund
Description: Individual assistance to children in need

Restrictions (for all programs): Limited to residents of Hawaii
$ Given: In 1989, 116 grants totaling $78,111 were awarded to individuals; range, $80 - $1,500; general range, $100 - $1,000; average, $680.
Application Information: Call for application guidelines; formal application required
Deadline: None
Contact: Suzanne Toguchi, Program Officer

PRIVATE FOUNDATION FUNDING

IDAHO

Rouch (A.P. and Louise) Boys Foundation
c/o Twin Falls Bank & Trust
Trust Department
P.O. Box 7
Twin Falls, ID 83303-0007
phone: N/A

Description: Financial assistance to needy children in the Magic Valley, Idaho, area. Assistance provided in the forms of medical care, clothing and summer camp fees
Restrictions: Limited to residents of the Magic Valley, Idaho area
$ Given: Grants range from $3 - $1,600.
Application Information: Write for guidelines
Deadline: N/A
Contact: N/A

ILLINOIS

Reade Industrial Fund
c/o Harris Trust and Savings Bank
P.O. Box 755
111 West Monroe Street
Chicago, IL 60690
(312) 461-7550

Description: Emergency loans or grants to individuals who are unable to care for themselves and/or their family members
Restrictions: Limited to individuals who are currently or who have previously been employed in industry in Illinois
$ Given: Grants range from $373 - $5,000.
Application Information: Initial approach by letter; formal application required
Deadline: None
Contact: Tony Abiera

. . . .

**Swiss Benevolent Society
of Chicago**
P.O. Box 2137
Chicago, IL 60690
phone: N/A

Description: Grants to elderly and other individuals of Swiss descent or nationality in cases of need or emergency
Restrictions: Limited to Chicago area residents of Swiss descent or nationality
$ Given: 55 grants totaling $53,450 are awarded to individuals.
Application Information: Formal application required; write for program information and current program deadlines
Deadline: Varies
Contact: Admiral Alan Weber, President

INDIANA

Mosette Levin Trust
c/o First Citizens Bank, N.A.
Trust Department
P.O. Box 1125
Michigan City, IN 46360
(800) 873-7001

Description: Medical aid grants to individuals over the age of 16 who are suffering from cancer or under the age of 16 who are suffering from any childhood illness. Funds may be used for treatment, medication, and transportation to and from treatment facility.
Restrictions: Limited to residents of La Porte County, Indiana
$ Given: In 1989, 20 grants totaling $11,120 were awarded to individuals; range, $20 - $1,630; general range, $20 - $1,000.
Application Information: Formal application required; interviews required
Deadline: None
Contact: N/A

. . . .

Mills (Allen & Rose) Trust
c/o Irwin Union Bank &
Trust Company
500 Washington Street
Columbus, IN 47201
phone: N/A

Description: Financial assistance to cancer patients, as well as to individuals with other medical problems and financial needs
Restrictions: Limited to residents of Bartholomew County, Indiana
$ Given: In 1989, five grants totaling $2,760 were awarded to individuals; range, $100 - $1,640.
Application Information: No direct applications accepted; requests referred to trustees by various social agencies
Deadline: None
Contact: Stephen Kirts

KANSAS

Charlotte Hill Charitable Trust
P.O. Box 754
Winfield, KS 67156
(316) 221-4600

Description: Grants to single women over age 60 with limited income and assets
Restrictions: Limited to residents of the Arkansas City and Winfield, Kansas, areas
$ Given: In FY89, 62 grants totaling $75,700 were awarded to individuals; range, $40 - $5,900.
Application Information: Formal application required
Deadline: None
Contact: Loyette Olson

Jones (Walter S. and Evan C.) Foundation
527 Commercial Street
Room 515
Emporia, KS 66801
(316) 342-1714
ADDITIONAL ADDRESS:
c/o Bank IV Emporia
Emporia, KS 66801

Description: Financial assistance for medical expenses. Grants based on demonstrated financial need
Restrictions: Applicants must have been continuous residents of Lyon, Coffey or Osage counties, Kansas, for at least one year; applicants must be under 21 years of age
$ Given: In FY89, 2,192 medical assistance grants totaling $625,074 were awarded to individuals; range, $60 - $6,173.
Application Information: Initial approach by letter; formal application required; interviews required; parents of applicant must submit comprehensive financial statement.
Deadline: Prior to beginning of medical services
Contact: Sharon R. Brown, General Manager

MAINE

Camden Home for Senior Citizens
66 Washington Street
Camden, ME 04843
(207) 236-2087
APPLICATION ADDRESS:
Belfast Road, Camden, ME
04843, (207) 236-2014

Description: Grants for medical care and drugs
Restrictions: Limited to residents of Camden, Rockport, Lincolnville, and Hope, Maine
$ Given: In FY89, 200 grants totaling $42,350 were awarded to individuals; range, $50 - $300.
Application Information: Write or call for guidelines
Deadline: None
Contact: Charles Lowe, President

Anita Card Montgomery Foundation
20 Mechanic Street
Camden, ME 04843-1707
phone: N/A

Description: Grants to needy individuals, including funding for medical and dental expenses
Restrictions: Limited to residents of Camden, Rockport, Lincolnville, and Hope, Maine
$ Given: Grants range from $40 - $4,060.
Application Information: Write for guidelines
Deadline: None
Contact: Robert C. Perkins

Portland Female Charitable Society
c/o Janet Matty
20 Noyes Street
Portland, ME 04103
phone: N/A
APPLICATION ADDRESS:
142 Pleasant Street
No. 761
Portland, ME 04101

Description: Financial aid for such needs as health care, food and shelter. Emphasis on the needs of children, the elderly, and the sick
Restrictions: Strictly limited to residents of Portland, Maine
$ Given: In FY89, 33 grants totaling $9,550 were awarded to individuals; range, $20 - $850.
Application Information: Full information required; applications usually presented by social workers, health care professionals, etc.; interviews required
Deadline: None
Contact: Janet Matty

PRIVATE FOUNDATION FUNDING

Herbert E. Wadsworth Trust
c/o Fleet Bank of Maine
Merrill Center
Exchange Street
Bangor, ME 04401
phone: N/A

Description: Financial assistance for citizens of Winthrop, Maine, who are hospitalized in a well-regulated and recognized facility outside the town of Winthrop
Restrictions: Limited to citizens of Winthrop, Maine
$ Given: In FY89, nine grants totaling $8,440 were awarded to individuals; range, $100 - $3,150.
Application Information: Write for guidelines
Deadline: None
Contact: N/A

MARYLAND

Anna Emory Warfield Memorial Fund, Inc.
103 West Monument Street
Baltimore, MD 21201
(301) 547-0612

Description: Relief assistance to elderly women in the Baltimore, Maryland area
Restrictions: Limited to women in the Baltimore, Maryland area
$ Given: In 1989, 42 grants totaling $150,000 were awarded to individuals; range, $900 - $3,925.
Application Information: Write to request application guidelines; formal application required
Deadline: None
Contact: Thelma K. O'Neal, Secretary

MASSACHUSETTS

The Pilgrim Foundation
478 Torrey Street
Brockton, MA 02401-4654
(508) 586-6100

Description: Financial assistance to families and children
Restrictions: Limited to residents of Brockton, Massachusetts
$ Given: Welfare assistance grants totaling $7,230 are awarded to individuals.
Application Information: Formal application required
Deadline: N/A
Contact: Executive Director

• •

Charlotte M. Robbins Trust

c/o State Street Bank &
Trust Company
P.O. Box 351
Boston, MA 02101
(617) 654-3360
APPLICATION ADDRESS:
c/o State Street Bank
225 Franklin Street
Boston, MA 02110

Description: Financial assistance to aged couples and aged women
Restrictions: Limited to aged residents of the towns of Groton, Ayer, Harvard, Shirley, and Littleton, Massachusetts
$ Given: In 1989, total giving was $6,000.
Application Information: Write letter to application address, stating income, expenses, assets, and reason money is needed
Deadline: N/A
Contact: Cheryl D. Curtin, Vice President

Salem Female Charitable Society

175 Federal Street
Boston, MA 02110
phone: N/A
APPLICATION ADDRESS:
30 Chestnut Street
Salem, MA 01970

Description: Grants to needy women of the Salem, Massachusetts, area
Restrictions: Original grant limited to residents of the Salem, Massachusetts, area. Recipients may, however, relocate without forfeiting grant.
$ Given: In FY89, 18 grants totaling $19,810 were awarded to individuals; range, $200 - $1,700; average, $800.
Application Information: Write for guidelines
Deadline: None
Contact: Jane A. Phillips, Treasurer

Shaw Fund for Mariners' Children

c/o Russell Brier &
Company
50 Congress Street
Room 800
Boston, MA 02109
phone: N/A
APPLICATION ADDRESS:
64 Concord Avenue
Norwood, MA 02062

Description: Grants to financially distressed mariners and their families
Restrictions: Limited to mariners, their wives or widows, and their children; Massachusetts residents only
$ Given: Grants totaling $114,140 are awarded to individuals.
Application Information: Write for program information
Deadline: None
Contact: Clare M. Tolias

PRIVATE FOUNDATION FUNDING

· ·

The Swasey Fund for Relief of Public School Teachers of Newburyport, Inc.
31 Milk Street
Boston, MA 02109
(508) 462-2784
APPLICATION ADDRESS:
23 Summit Place
Newburyport, MA 01950

Description: Financial aid to individuals who have taught in the Newburyport, Massachusetts public school system for at least 10 years
Restrictions: See above
$ Given: In FY89, 21 grants totaling $66,600 were awarded to individuals; range, $100 - $10,000.
Application Information: Formal application required
Deadline: None
Contact: Jean MacDonald, Treasurer

Urann Foundation
P.O. Box 1788
Brockton, MA 02403
(508) 588-7744

Description: Medical assistance grants for Massachusetts families engaged in cranberry farming and processing. Grants intended to assist in payment of hospital and medical bills
Restrictions: Limited to families located in Massachusetts
$ Given: In 1989, 22 grants totaling $44,460 were awarded to individuals; 1 medical assistance grant for $680 was awarded.
Application Information: Initial contact by phone or letter
Deadline: None
Contact: Howard Whelan, Administrator

MINNESOTA

Hanna R. Kristianson Trust
P.O. Box 1011
Albert Lea, MN 56007
APPLICATION ADDRESS:
Clarks Grove, MN 56016
(507) 256-4415

Description: Financial aid to needy individuals over 50 years of age
Restrictions: Limited to residents of Freeborn County, Minnesota who are over 50 years old
$ Given: Grants range from $20 - $1,660.
Application Information: Call or write for guidelines
Deadline: None
Contact: Richard S. Haug, Trustee

• • • • • • • • • • • • • • • • • • • •

**Charles D. Gilfillan
Paxton Memorial, Inc.**
c/o Thomas W. Murray,
Vice President
W-555 First National Bank
Building
St. Paul, MN 55101
(612) 291-6236
APPLICATION ADDRESS:
Committee of Beneficiaries
200 Southwest First Street
Rochester, MN 55905
(507) 282-2511

Description: Medical assistance to financially distressed Minnesota residents; priority given to those in rural areas and towns with populations of less than 3,000
Restrictions: Limited to residents of Minnesota
$ Given: In FY89, 80 grants totaling $39,900 were awarded to individuals; range, $38 - $2,160; average, $500.
Application Information: Formal application required
Deadline: None
Contact: Marie LaPlante, Secretary

**The Saint Paul
Foundation**
1120 Norwest Center
St. Paul, MN 55101
(612) 224-5463

Description: Relief assistance grants
Restrictions: Limited to residents of St. Paul and Minneapolis, Minnesota, and to employees of 3M Company
$ Given: 15 relief assistance grants totaling $42,504 are awarded to individuals.
Application Information: Write or call for guidelines
Deadline: N/A
Contact: Paul A. Verret, President

MISSOURI

**Herschend Family
Foundation**
c/o Jack R. Herschend
Silver Dollar City, Inc.
Branson, MO 65616
(417) 338-2611

Description: Assistance for individuals in need
Restrictions: Intended primarily for residents of Missouri
$ Given: In 1989, 34 grants totaling $250,430 were awarded to individuals.
Application Information: Call or write, explaining need
Deadline: None
Contact: Jack R. Herschend, Director

PRIVATE FOUNDATION FUNDING

• •

NEW HAMPSHIRE

Abbie M. Griffin Hospital Fund
111 Concord Street
Nashua, NH 03060
phone: N/A

Description: Grants for payment of hospital bills
Restrictions: Limited to residents of Merrimack, Hillsborough County, New Hampshire
$ Given: Four grants totaling $11,000 are awarded to individuals; range, $2,221 - $3,370.
Application Information: Write for guidelines
Deadline: None
Contact: S. Robert Winer, Trustee

Ida E. Walton Trust
189 Union Avenue
Laconia, NH 03246
phone: N/A
APPLICATION ADDRESS:
c/o Paul L. Normandin
Trustee
213 Union Avenue
Laconia, NH 03246

Description: Grants for medical care for needy children
Restrictions: Limited to residents of New Hampshire
$ Given: In 1989, 12 grants totaling $2,020 were awarded to individuals; range, $40 - $500.
Application Information: Send a written request, informing trustees of applicant's needs
Deadline: N/A
Contact: Paul L. Normandin, Trustee

NEW JERSEY

The de Kay Foundation
c/o Manufacturers Hanover Trust Company
270 Park Avenue
New York, NY 10017
(212) 270-6000

Description: Grants to elderly individuals in financial need, particularly to those who are sick or disabled or who lack proper care
Restrictions: Limited to residents of New York, New Jersey and Connecticut
$ Given: In FY89, 83 grants totaling $202,540 were awarded to individuals; range, $350 - $7,150; general range, $1,000 - $5,000.
Application Information: Initial approach by letter; formal application required
Deadline: None
Contact: Lloyd Saltus II, Vice President

Otto Sussman Trust
P.O. Box 1374
Trainsmeadow Station
Flushing, NY 11370-9998
phone: N/A

Description: Financial assistance for medical bills and caregiving expenses to individuals with serious or terminal illnesses
Restrictions: Limited to residents of New York, New Jersey, Oklahoma, and Pennsylvania
$ Given: Grants range from $329 - $4,000.
Application Information: Write letter requesting application form and guidelines; explain circumstances of need; formal application required
Deadline: None
Contact: Edward S. Miller, Trustee

NEW YORK

The James Gordon Bennett Memorial Corporation
c/o New York Daily News
220 East 42nd Street
New York, NY 10017
phone: N/A

Description: Grants to journalists who have been employees of a daily New York City newspaper for ten years or more. Acceptance based on need. Funds to be used for "the physical needs of persons . . . who, by reason of old age, accident or bodily infirmity, or through lack of means, are unable to care for themselves."
Restrictions: Priority given to journalists who have worked in the borough of Manhattan
$ Given: Grants range from $150 - $6,000.
Application Information: Write for guidelines and program information; formal application required
Deadline: None
Contact: Denise Houseman

Brockway Foundation for the Needy of the Village and Township of Homer, New York
c/o Key Bank
25 South Main Street
Homer, NY 13077-1314
phone: N/A

Description: Financial assistance based on need
Restrictions: Limited to residents of the Homer, New York, area
$ Given: Grants range from $180 - $600.
Application Information: Write for guidelines
Deadline: None
Contact: M. Lee Swartwout, Treasurer

PRIVATE FOUNDATION FUNDING

The Clark Foundation
30 Wall Street
New York, NY 10005
(212) 269-1833

Description: Financial aid for medical and hospital care to needy individuals in upstate New York and New York City
Restrictions: Limited to residents of upstate New York and New York City
$ Given: In FY89, 18 grants totaling $108,330 were awarded to individuals; range, $560 - $15,600.
Application Information: Write for guidelines
Deadline: None
Contact: Edward W. Stack, Secretary

Josiah H. Danforth Memorial Fund
8 Fremont Street
Gloversville, NY 12078
phone: N/A

Description: Financial aid for medical care
Restrictions: Limited to residents of Fulton County, New York
$ Given: In 1989, 95 grants totaling $18,610 were awarded to individuals; range, $16 - $500; average, $200; maximum grant per year per person, $500.
Application Information: Write for guidelines, application form; formal application required
Deadline: None
Contact: N/A

The de Kay Foundation
c/o Manufacturers Hanover Trust Company
270 Park Avenue
New York, NY 10020
(212) 270-6000

Description: Grants to elderly individuals in financial need, particularly to those who are sick or disabled or who lack proper care
Restrictions: Limited to residents of New York, New Jersey and Connecticut
$ Given: In FY89, 83 grants totaling $202,540 were awarded to individuals; range, $350 - $7,150; general range, $1,000 - $5, 000.
Application Information: Initial approach by letter; formal application required
Deadline: None
Contact: Lloyd Saltus II, Vice President

· · · · · · · · · · · · · · · · · · · ·

Mary W. MacKinnon Fund
c/o Wilber National Bank
Trust Department
245 Main Street
Oneonta, NY 13820
phone: N/A

Description: Funding for medical, hospital, nursing home, and rehabilitative care for elderly and indigent residents of Sidney, New York
Restrictions: Limited to residents of Sidney, New York
$ Given: Grants totaling $48,453 are awarded to individuals.
Application Information: Applications must be submitted through a physician or hospital
Deadline: None
Contact: N/A

Saranac Lake Voluntary Health Association, Inc.
70 Main Street
Saranac Lake, NY 12983-1706
phone: N/A

Description: Provides funding for visiting nurse services for the elderly in Saranac Lake, New York, as well as grants for dental services to students
Restrictions: Limited to residents of Saranac Lake, New York
$ Given: In FY89, 3 grants totaling $42,120 were awarded to individuals; range, $4,498 - $31,613.
Application Information: Write for guidelines
Deadline: N/A
Contact: N/A

St. Luke's Nurses Benefit Fund
47 Phillips Lane
Darien, CT 06820
phone: N/A

Description: Grants for needy graduates of St. Luke's School of Nursing
Restrictions: Limited to St. Luke's alumnae
$ Given: In FY89, one grant for $2,000 was awarded.
Application Information: Formal application required
Deadline: None
Contact: Martha Kirk, Trustee

PRIVATE FOUNDATION FUNDING

· ·

Suffolk County Happy Landing Fund, Inc.
c/o Peter Opromolla
Box 383
St. James, NY 11780
(516) 366-4843

Decription: Financial assistance to police officers and their families in Suffolk County, New York. Grants or loans given only to police officers in extreme financial difficulties
Restrictions: Limited to police officers in Suffolk County, New York
$ Given: In FY90, three grants of $1,000 each were awarded to individuals.
Application Information: Initial approach must be made by a superior officer. Formal application required; interviews required. Write or call for informational brochure.
Deadline: None
Contact: Peter Opromolla

Otto Sussman Trust
P.O. Box 1374
Trainsmeadow Station
Flushing, NY 11370-9998
phone: N/A

Description: Financial assistance for medical bills and caregiving expenses to individuals with serious or terminal illnesses
Restrictions: Limited to residents of New York, New Jersey, Oklahoma, and Pennsylvania
$ Given: Grants range from $329 - $4,000.
Application Information: Write letter requesting application form and guidelines; explain circumstances of need; formal application required
Deadline: None
Contact: Edward S. Miller, Trustee

VonderLinden Charitable Trust
c/o Leonard Rachmilowitz
26 Mill Street
Rhinebeck, NY 12572
(914) 876-3021

Description: Grants for financially distressed residents of upstate New York. Funds may be used to meet a variety of needs, including medical bills
Restrictions: Limited to residents of upstate New York
$ Given: In FY89, 101 grants totaling $23,260 were awarded to individuals; range, $4 - $540.
Application Information: Write or call for guidelines
Deadline: None
Contact: Leonard Rachmilowitz

• • • • • • • • • • • • • • • • • • • •

NORTH CAROLINA

Community Foundation of Gaston County, Inc.
(formerly Garrison Community Foundation of Gaston County, Inc.)
P.O. Box 123
Gastonia, NC 28053
(704) 864-0927

Description: Grants for medical expenses only
Restrictions: Limited to children, age 18 and younger, who are residents of Gaston County, North Carolina
$ Given: An unspecified number of grants totaling $9,000 are awarded to individuals.
Application Information: Write for guidelines and application forms; formal application required; interviews required
Deadline: None
Contact: Harold T. Sumner, Executive Director

OHIO

Christian BusinessCares Foundation
P.O. Box 360691
Cleveland, OH 44136
(216) 621-0096

Description: One time grants for life-threatening medical emergencies
Restrictions: Limited to residents of northeast Ohio. Awards determined on basis of the effect of grant on applicant's overall condition
$ Given: Grants range from $8 - $10,000; average, $270.
Application Information: Write for guidelines, brochure and newsletter; formal application required; interviews required
Deadline: None
Contact: N/A

Columbus Female Benevolent Society
228 South Drexel Avenue
Columbus, OH 43209
phone: N/A

Description: Direct aid to pensioned widows
Restrictions: Limited to widows who are residents of Franklin County, Ohio
$ Given: In 1989, an unspecified number of grants totaling $32,800 were awarded to individuals.
Application Information: No direct applications; recipients are referred by people in the community who are familiar with their circumstances
Deadline: N/A
Contact: N/A

PRIVATE FOUNDATION FUNDING

. . . .

The Ford (S.N. and Ada) Fund
c/o Society Bank & Trust
P.O. Box 849
Mansfield, OH 44901
(419) 525-7676

Description: Grants for hospitalization and care of the aged and incurably ill
Restrictions: Limited to residents of Richland County, Ohio
$ Given: Grants range from $23 - $11,470.
Application Information: Write for guidelines and annual report
Deadline: N/A
Contact: Nick Gesouras, Regional Trust Officer

Meshech Frost Testamentary Trust
109 South Washington
Street, Tiffin, OH 44883
phone: N/A

Description: Grants to Tiffin, Ohio residents who are in financial need
Restrictions: Limited to residents of Tiffin, Ohio
$ Given: Grants range from $169 - $690.
Application Information: Submit letter stating reasons for request
Deadline: None
Contact: Kenneth H. Myers, Secretary-Treasurer

James R. Nicholl Memorial Foundation
c/o The Central Trust
Company of Northern Ohio
Trust Department
1949 Broadway
Lorain, OH 44052
(216) 244-1965

Description: Financial assistance for medical and surgical services to needy children (2 to 21 years of age). Grants paid directly to health care providers
Restrictions: Limited to children who have been residents of Lorain County, Ohio for at least two years
$ Given: In 1989, 11 medical assistance grants totaling $26,550 were awarded to individuals; range, $14 - $4,040.
Application Information: Write for informational brochure and application guidelines; indicate medical need; formal application required
Deadline: None
Contact: David E. Nocjar, Trust Officer

• • • • • • • • • • • • • • • • •

Virginia Wright Mothers Guild, Inc.
426 Clinton Street
Columbus, OH 43202-2741
phone: N/A

Description: Grants to aged women in financial need
Restrictions: Strictly limited to female residents of Columbus, Ohio
$ Given: Grants totaling $9,924 are awarded to individuals.
Application Information: Write for guidelines
Deadline: N/A
Contact: M. Courtwright

OKLAHOMA

Otto Sussman Trust
P.O. Box 1374
Trainsmeadow Station
Flushing, NY 11370-9998
phone: N/A

Description: Financial assistance for medical bills and caregiving expenses to individuals with serious or terminal illnesses
Restrictions: Limited to residents of New York, New Jersey, Oklahoma, and Pennsylvania
$ Given: Grants range from $329 - $4,000.
Application Information: Write letter requesting application form and guidelines; explain circumstances of need; formal application required
Deadline: None
Contact: Edward S. Miller, Trustee

OREGON

The Elizabeth Church Clarke Testamentary Trust/Fund Foundation
U.S. National Bank of Oregon
P.O. Box 3168
Portland, OR 97208
(503) 228-9405
APPLICATION ADDRESS:
Scottish Rite Temple
709 S.W. 15th Avenue
Portland, OR 97205

Description: Grants for medical assistance. Payments may be made directly to the individuals or to the physicians and hospitals providing services.
Restrictions: Limited to residents of Oregon
$ Given: In 1989, total giving was $32,770.
Application Information: Initial approach by letter, detailing needs and costs
Deadline: None
Contact: G.L. Selmyhr, Executive Secretary

PRIVATE FOUNDATION FUNDING

**Clarke (Louis G. &
Elizabeth L.) Endowment
Fund**
U.S. National Bank of
Oregon
P.O. Box 3168
Portland, OR 97208
(503) 228-9405
APPLICATION ADDRESS:
Scottish Rite Temple
709 S.W. 15th Avenue
Portland, OR 97205

Description: Grants to needy Masons or their immediate family who require hospitalization in the Portland, Oregon metropolitan area (Multnomah, Clackamas and Washington counties)
Restrictions: Limited to Masons and their immediate families
$ Given: In FY89, an unspecified number of grants totaling $34,380 were awarded to individuals.
Application Information: Write for guidelines
Deadline: N/A
Contact: G.L. Selmyhr, Executive Secretary

**Blanche Fischer
Foundation**
1001 South West Fifth
Avenue
Suite 1550
Portland, OR 97204
(503) 323-9111

Description: Financial aid for physically handicapped persons in Oregon
Restrictions: Limited to Oregon residents who have demonstrated financial need and who are disabled or physically handicapped
$ Given: In 1989, 148 grants totaling $70,190 were awarded to individuals; range, $25 - $1,500; general range, $100 - $1,000; average, $410.
Application Information: Write for application guidelines; formal application required
Deadline: None
Contact: William K. Shepherd, President

**Sophia Byers McComas
Foundation**
c/o U.S. National Bank of
Oregon
P.O. Box 3168
Portland, OR 97208
(503) 275-6564

Description: Grants to elderly and indigent residents of Oregon who are not receiving welfare assistance
Restrictions: Limited to residents of Oregon
$ Given: In FY89, an unspecified number of grants totaling $72,222 were awarded to individuals.
Application Information: Individuals may not apply directly; applicants are recommended to the trustees by various church groups, service agencies, etc.
Deadline: N/A
Contact: U.S. National Bank of Oregon, Trustee

Scottish Rite Oregon Consistory Almoner Fund, Inc.
Scottish Rite Temple
709 S.W. 15th Avenue
Portland, OR 97205
(503) 228-9405

Description: Assistance to financially distressed Masons and their families to help meet medical expenses
Restrictions: Limited to Masons and their wives, widows and childrenwho are residents of the state of Oregon
$ Given: In FY89, an unspecified number of grants totaling $19,440 were awarded to individuals.
Application Information: Write for guidelines
Deadline: None
Contact: Walter Peters

PENNSYLVANIA

Margaret Baker Memorial Fund Trust
Mellon Bank (East) N.A.
P.O. Box 7236
Philadelphia, PA 19101-7236
phone: N/A
APPLICATION ADDRESS:
P.O. Box 663, Phoenixville, PA 19460

Description: Financial aid to widows and single women over age 30 and handicapped children under age 14
Restrictions: Limited to residents of the Phoenixville, Pennsylvania, area
$ Given: Grants range from $108 - $750.
Application Information: Send a letter including the applicant's age, income, infirmity (if any), and other supportive material, plus the name of a person who can verify the request
Deadline: Applications accepted throughout the year; awards are usually made in July and November
Contact: L. Darlington Lessig, Treasurer

PRIVATE FOUNDATION FUNDING

Addison H. Gibson Foundation
Six PPG Place
Suite 860
Pittsburgh, PA 15222
(412) 261-1611

Description: Funds to cover hospital and medical costs for individuals with, "correctible physical difficulties"
Restrictions: Limited to residents of western Pennsylvania (with emphasis on Allegheny County
$ Given: Grants range from $60 - $12,000.
Application Information: Applicants must be referred by a medical professional. Formal application required. Medical professional must provide name, age, sex, and address of person for whom funding is sought, describe the nature of recommended medical assistance, and provide the name of the patient's primary physician. Grants are made directly to the medical professionals/institution providing services. Write for further information; formal application required; interviews required.
Deadline: None
Contact: Charlotte G. Kisseleff, Secretary

Edward W. Helfrick Senior Citizens Trust
400 Market Street
Sunbury, PA 17801
phone: N/A

Description: Grants to senior citizens of the 107th Legislative District in Pennsylvania who are in need as a result of fire or illness
Restrictions: See above
$ Given: Four grants of $500 each were awarded to individuals.
Application Information: Write for guidelines
Deadline: None
Contact: N/A

• • • • • • • • • • • • • • •

William B. Lake Foundation
Fidelity Bank, N.A.
Broad & Walnut Streets
3MBO
Philadelphia, PA 19109
(215) 985-7320

Description: Aid to individuals suffering from respiratory diseases
Restrictions: Limited to residents of the Philadelphia, Pennsylvania, area
$ Given: In FY90, an unspecified number of grants totaling $30,000 were awarded to individuals.
Application Information: Initial approach by letter; please include details of physical condition and supporting documents
Deadlines: May 1 and November 1
Contact: Maureen B. Evans, Secretary-Treasurer

Quin (Robert D. & Margaret W.) Foundation
Hazleton National Bank
101 West Broad Street
Hazleton, PA 18201
phone: N/A

Description: Grants for students in financial need; intended to meet needs including medication costs
Restrictions: Limited to individuals up to 19 years old who are at least one-year residents of an area within a 10-mile radius of the Hazleton, Pennsylvania City Hall
$ Given: Grants range from $35 - $900.
Application Information: Write for guidelines
Deadline: None
Contact: N/A

Otto Sussman Trust
P.O. Box 1374
Trainsmeadow Station
Flushing, NY 11370-9998
phone: N/A

Description: Financial assistance for medical bills and caregiving expenses to individuals with serious or terminal illnesses
Restrictions: Limited to residents of New York, New Jersey, Oklahoma, and Pennsylvania
$ Given: Grants range from $329 - $4,000.
Application Information: Write letter requesting application form and guidelines; explain circumstances of need; formal application required
Deadline: None
Contact: Edward S. Miller, Trustee

41

RHODE ISLAND

Bristol Home for Aged Women
c/o Rhode Island
Hospital Trust Bank
One Hospital Trust Plaza
Providence, RI 02903
(401) 278-8752

Description: Financial aid for elderly, needy women
Restrictions: Limited to residents of Bristol, Rhode Island
$ Given: In FY89, eight grants totaling $9,310 were awarded to individuals; range, $100 - $4,900.
Application Information: Initial approach by letter; letter should include cost and description of service needed
Deadline: June 1
Contact: Mr. Shawn P. Buckless, Assistant Vice President

Robert B. Cranston/ Theophilus T. Pitman Fund
18 Market Square
Newport, RI 02840
(401) 847-4260

Description: Grants to the aged, temporarily indigent and indigent people of Newport County, Rhode Island. Funds for medical assistance, food, utilities, clothing and housing
Restrictions: Limited to residents of Newport County, Rhode Island
$ Given: In FY89, an unspecified number of grants totaling $6,850 were awarded to individuals.
Application Information: Interview or reference from a local welfare agency required
Deadline: None
Contact: The Reverend D.C. Hambly, Jr., Administrator

Inez Sprague Trust
c/o Rhode Island
Hospital Trust Bank
One Hospital Trust Plaza
Providence, RI 02903
(401) 278-8700

Description: Financial assistance and medical expenses for needy individuals
Restrictions: Limited to residents of Rhode Island
$ Given: In FY89, 23 grants totaling $6,000 were awarded to individuals; range, $79 - $1,500.
Application Information: Initial approach by letter
Deadline: None
Contact: Trustee

• • • • • • • • • • • • • • • • • • • •

SOUTH CAROLINA

Graham Memorial Fund
308 West Main Street
Bennettsville, SC 29512
(803) 479-6804

Description: Grants for medical assistance and general welfare
Restrictions: Limited to residents of Bennettsville, South Carolina
$ Given: In FY89, 37 grants totaling $11,200 were awarded to individuals; range, $200 - $500.
Application Information: Formal application required
Deadline: June 1
Contact: Chairman

TENNESSEE

State Industries Foundation
P.O. Box 307
Old Ferry Road
Ashland City, TN 37015
(615) 244-7040

Description: Financial assistance to needy individuals in Tennessee, including State Industries employees
Restrictions: Limited to residents of Tennessee
$ Given: Grants range from $1 - $400; average, $150.
Application Information: Write or call for guidelines
Deadline: None
Contact: Joseph P. Lanier, Manager

TEXAS

Dallas Cotton Exchange Trust
Dallas Cotton Exchange
c/o Mr. Joe Ferguson
Dixon Trust Company
3141 Hood Street
Suite 600
Dallas, TX 75219
phone: N/A

Description: Financial aid to persons engaged or formerly engaged in the cotton merchandising business in Dallas, Texas, their employees and former employees, and the immediate families of the above — when they are unable to work or, if able to work, unable to earn a sufficient amount to meet their needs
Restrictions: See above
$ Given: Grants range from $1,750 - $3,300.
Application Information: Formal application required
Deadline: None
Contact: Joe Ferguson

PRIVATE FOUNDATION FUNDING

· · · · · · · · · · · · · · · · · · · ·

H.C. Davis Fund
P.O. Box 2239
San Antonio, TX 78298
phone: N/A

Description: Grants to assist infirm Masons living in the 39th Masonic District of Texas
Restrictions: (see above)
$ Given: Grants range from $200 - $3,075.
Application Information: Write for guidelines
Deadline: None
Contact: N/A

F.V. Hall, Jr. & Marylou Hall Children's Crisis Foundation
c/o NCNB Texas National Bank
P.O. Box 830241
Dallas, TX 75283-0241
phone: N/A

Description: Assistance to infants and children in crisis, or a situation of critical need or critical want
Restrictions: Limited to children under the age of 12, either born in Tom Green County, Texas, or who have been physically in residence for more than 12 consecutive months, and whose parents or guardians have no financial sources available to meet the child's needs
$ Given: In FY89, an unspecified number of grants totaling $80,400 were awarded to individuals.
Application Information: Formal application required; interviews sometimes required
Deadline: None
Contact: Alice J. Gayle, Trust Officer, NCNB Texas National Bank

The Kings Foundation
P.O. Box 27333
Austin, TX 78755
phone: N/A

Description: Grants to individuals in financial need
Restrictions: Intended primarily for residents of Texas
$ Given: Grants range from $50 - $250.
Application Information: Initial approach by letter
Deadline: N/A
Contact: N/A

• • • • • • • • • • • • • • • • • • • •

Pardee Cancer Treatment Association of Greater Brazosport
127-C Circle Way
Lake Jackson, TX 77566
phone: N/A

Description: Financial aid for treatment of cancer
Restrictions: Limited to residents of Southern Brazoria County, Texas
$ Given: An unspecified number of grants totaling $100,645 are awarded to individuals.
Application Information: Formal application required
Deadline: None
Contact: Shirley Funk

Sunnyside Foundation, Inc.
8609 Northwest Plaza Drive
Suite 201
Dallas, TX 75225
(214) 692-5686

Description: Short-term assistance to underprivileged children for their physical, moral and spiritual needs, including general welfare aid and camperships
Restrictions: Limited to residents of Texas
$ Given: Grants range from $39 - $4,350.
Application Information: Formal application required
Deadline: None
Contact: Mary Rothenflue, Executive Director

VIRGINIA

A.C. Needles Trust Fund Hospital Care
c/o Dominion Trust Company
P.O. Box 13327
Roanoke, VA 24040
phone: N/A

Description: Grants for hospital care to financially distressed individuals
Restrictions: Limited to individuals in the Roanoke, Virginia, area
$ Given: Grants range from $710 - $9,450.
Application Information: Write for guidelines
Deadline: N/A
Contact: N/A

PRIVATE FOUNDATION FUNDING

. . . .

WASHINGTON

G.M.L. Foundation, Inc.
P.O. Box 848
Port Angeles, WA 98362
phone: N/A

Description: Grants to individuals who need medical help
Restrictions: Limited to residents of Clallam County, Washington
$ Given: Grants totaling $12,275 are awarded to individuals.
Application Information: Write for guidelines
Deadline: N/A
Contact: Graham Ralston, Secretary

George T. Welch Testamentary Trust
c/o Baker-Boyer National Bank
P.O. Box 1796
Walla Walla, WA 99362
(509) 525-2000

Description: Medical assistance for financially distressed individuals
Restrictions: Limited to residents of Walla Walla County, Washington
$ Given: In FY89, 29 welfare assistance grants totaling $21,980 were awarded to individuals; range, $53 - $1,500.
Application Information: Formal application required
Deadlines: February 20, May 20, August 20, November 20
Contact: Bettie Loiacono, Trust Officer

WEST VIRGINIA

Good Shepherd Foundation, Inc.
Route 4
Box 349
Kinston, NC 28501-9317
(919) 569-3241

Description: Financial assistance for medical expenses
Restrictions: Limited to residents of Trent Township, West Virginia
$ Given: Grants range from $1,130 - $2,500.
Application Information: Initial approach by letter; formal application required
Deadline: None
Contact: Sue White, Secretary-Treasurer

Jamey Harless Foundation, Inc.
Drawer D
Gilbert, WV 25621
(304) 664-3227

Description: Loans and grants to financially distressed families
Restrictions: Limited to residents of the Gilbert, West Virginia, area
$ Given: Distress grants totaling $4,720 are awarded to individuals; distress loans totaling $5,600 are made to individuals.
Application Information: Initial approach by letter; formal application required
Deadline: None
Contact: Sharon Murphy, Secretary

WISCONSIN

Edward Rutledge Charity
P.O. Box 758
Chippewa Falls, WI 54729
(715) 723-6618

Description: Grants and loans to needy residents of Chippewa County, Wisconsin
Restrictions: (see above)
$ Given: In FY90, 235 relief assistance grants totaling $16,285 were awarded to individuals; range, $5 - $600.
Application Information: Formal application required
Deadline: July 1
Contact: John Frampton, President

WYOMING

The Gorgen (Peter and Anna) Fund Charitable Trust
141 South Main Street
Buffalo, WY 82834-1824
(307) 684-2211
ADDITIONAL ADDRESS: c/o William J. Kirven, 104 Fort Street, Buffalo, WY 82834
(307) 684-2248

Description: Financial assistance for medical, dental and optical services. Grants paid directly to provider of services
Restrictions: Limited to children in Johnson County, Wyoming
$ Given: Grants range from $16 - $500; average, $100.
Application Information: Write for guidelines
Deadline: None
Contact: Robert R. Holt, Trustee

PRIVATE FOUNDATION FUNDING

. . . .

Perkins (B.F. & Rose H.) Foundation
P.O. Box 1064
Sheridan, WY 82801
(307) 674-8871

Description: Funding for medical assistance to persons ages 2 to 20
Restrictions: Limited to individuals who have been residents of Sheridan County, Wyoming for the last two consecutive years, and who are between ages 2 and 20
$ Given: In 1989, 165 medical assistance grants totaling $50,097 were awarded to individuals; range, $21 - $1,800; general range, $25 - $1,000.
Application Information: Formal application required; obtain application forms from foundation; foundation will send separate form directly to attending physician for cost estimate; interviews required
Deadline: Applications accepted throughout the year; completed application form must be submitted by individual and attending physician by the first week of the month prior to treatment
Contact: Margaret Sweem, Manager

PRIVATE FOUNDATION FUNDING, NO GEOGRAPHICAL RESTRICTIONS

Bendheim (Charles and Els) Foundation
One Parker Plaza
Fort Lee, NJ 07024
phone: N/A

Description: Grants to individuals for charitable purposes, including aid to the sick and destitute
Restrictions: Applicants must be Jewish and in need of financial assistance
$ Given: In 1989, total giving was $171,880.
Application Information: Write for guidelines
Deadline: N/A
Contact: N/A

Broadcasters Foundation, Inc.
320 West 57th Street
New York, NY 10019
(212) 586-2000

Description: Grants to needy members of the broadcast industry and their families
Restrictions: (see above)
$ Given: Grants range from $1,800 - $2,400.
Application Information: Formal application required
Deadline: None
Contact: N/A

• • • • • • • • • • • • • • • • • •

Eagles Memorial Foundation, Inc.
4710 14th Street West
Bradenton, FL 34207
phone: N/A

Description: Grants to children of deceased Eagles servicemen and women, law officers and firefighters — for dental, medical and hospital expenses
Restrictions: Limited to children (under the age of 18, unmarried and not self-supporting) of members of the Fraternal Order of Eagles and the Ladies Auxiliary who have died from injuries or diseases incurred or aggravated while serving (1) in the armed forces, (2) as a law enforcement officer, or (3) as a full-time or volunteer firefighter. Individual recipients receive funds for psychiatric, hospital or orthodontic bills, total not to exceed $5,000. No benefits paid for self-inflicted injuries, crime-related injuries, or illnesses/injuries related to drug or alcohol abuse.
$ Given: In FY88, an unspecified number of medical assistance grants totaling $13,420 were awarded to individuals.
Application Information: Write for guidelines
Deadline: N/A
Contact: N/A

Island Memorial Medical Fund, Inc.
c/o Richard Purinon
Main Road
Washington Island, WI 54246
phone: N/A

Description: Financial assistance to help cover medical expenses for needy individuals. Funds paid directly to physicians or treatment facilities.
Restrictions: N/A
$ Given: Grants range from $630 - $8,760.
Application Information: Write foundation for application guidelines and current deadline information
Deadline: Varies
Contact: Richard Purinon

PRIVATE FOUNDATION FUNDING

Jockey Club Foundation
40 East 52nd Street
New York, NY 10022
(212) 371-5970

Description: Grants to financially distressted individuals who are legitimately connected with thoroughbred breeding and racing
Restrictions: See above
$ Given: In 1989, a total of $394,278 was awarded in grants to individuals.
Application Information: Write for program information and application guidelines.
Deadline: None
Contact: Nancy Colletti, Secretary to the Trustees

Max Mainzer Memorial Foundation, Inc.
570 Seventh Avenue
Third Floor
New York, NY 10018
(212) 921-3865

Description: Grants to financially distressed members of the American Jewish KC Fraternity or their widows
Restrictions: (see above)
$ Given: In FY89, 15 grants totaling $34,440 were awarded to individuals; range, $250 - $4,200.
Application Information: Contact foundation for guidelines
Deadline: None
Contact: N/A

NFL Alumni Foundation Fund
c/o Sigmund M. Hyman
P.O. Box 248
Stevenson, MD 21153-0248
(301) 486-5454

Description: Financial assistance to disabled former National Football League alumni (prior to 1959), including grants for death benefits and medical expenses
Restrictions: (see above)
$ Given: 24 grants totaling $144,420 are awarded to individuals; eligible persons may receive grants that will supplement their total annual income by up to $12,000, with a $250/month minimum.
Application Information: Initial approach by letter
Deadline: None
Contact: N/A

• • • • • • • • • • • • • • • • • • •

Katharine C. Pierce Trust
c/o State Street Bank &
Trust Company
P.O. Box 351
Boston, MA 02101
(617) 654-3357

Description: Financial assistance for needy women
Restrictions: See above
$ Given: In 1989, an unspecified number of grants totaling $33,500 were awarded to individuals; range, $250 - $5,000; general range, $1,000 - $5,000.
Application Information: Initial approach by letter, include personal history, needs and financial condition
Deadline: None
Contact: Robert W. Seymour, Trust Officer

Corporate/ Employee Grants

· ·

This chapter contains information about companies and corporations that provide grants or loans for their employees or former employees.

As in the chapter on Private Foundation Funding, the material is organized by state. In some cases, where a corporation has offices in several states, the corporation is listed only under the state in which its headquarters are located. Unless specificied in the restrictions, this does *not* mean that monies are available only to employees within that state. Wherever possible, each listing includes a description of what the foundation funds, any restrictions, the total amount of money awarded annually, the number of grants or loans made annually, the range of monies given, the average size of an award, information on how to apply, deadline date(s), and name(s) of contact person(s).

If your company/corporation is not included in this chapter, check with an employee benefits representative or your personnel director to see if your company offers assistance in paying medical expenses.

CORPORATE/EMPLOYEE GRANTS

• • • • • • • • • • • • • • • • • • • •

ARRANGED BY STATE, ACCORDING TO CORPORATE LOCATION

ALABAMA

The Stockham (William H. and Kate F.) Foundation, Inc.
c/o Stockham Valves &
Fittings, Inc.
4000 North Tenth Avenue
P.O. Box 10326
Birmingham, AL 35202
phone: N/A

Description: Need-based grants
Restrictions: Strictly limited to Stockham Valves &
Fittings, Inc. employees, former employees, and their
dependents
$ Given: Grants range from $150 - $9,555.
Application Information: Initial contact by letter
Deadline: None
Contact: Herbert Stockham, Chairman

CALIFORNIA

A.P. Giannini Foundation for Employees
c/o Bank of America
Personnel Relations
Department No. 3650
P.O. Box 37000
San Francisco, CA 94137
(415) 622-3706

Description: Relief grants to help cover medical bills
and other emergency expenses
Restrictions: Limited to Bank of America employees and
their families, and to employees of Bank of America
subsidiaries
$ Given: Three grants totaling $5,366 are awarded to
individuals; range, $787 - $2,640.
Application Information: Submit letter of application,
including reason for grant request, amount requested,
and assessment of applicant's financial status
Deadline: None
Contact: N/A

Clorinda Giannini Memorial Benefit Fund
c/o Bank of America
Trust Department
P.O. Box 37121
San Francisco, CA 94137
(415) 622-3650

Description: Emergency assistance grants for illness,
accident disability, surgery, medical and nursing care,
hospitalization, financial difficulties, and loss of income
Restrictions: Limited to Bank of America employees
$ Given: 25 grants totaling $27,926 are awarded to
individuals; range, $35 - $6,226; general range, $800 -
$2,000.
Application Information: Initial contact by letter
Deadline: None
Contact: Susan Morales

• • • • • • • • • • • • • • • • • • • •

George S. Ladd Memorial Fund
c/o V.M. Edwards
633 Folsom Street
Room 420
San Francisco, CA 94107
phone: N/A

Description: Financial assistance grants, including funding for medical treatment
Restrictions: Limited to elderly and retired employees of Pacific Bell, Nevada Bell and Pacific Northwest Bell
$ Given: Grants range from $1,271 - $4,450.
Application Information: Write for guidelines
Deadline: N/A
Contact: N/A

Pfaffinger Foundation
Times Mirror Square
Los Angeles, CA 90053
(213) 237-5743

Description: Need-based grants
Restrictions: Limited to employees and former employees of The Times Mirror Company
$ Given: Grants range from $13 - $40,553.
Application Information: Initial contact by letter; formal application required; final notification usually in one week after application is received
Deadline: None
Contact: James C. Kelly, President

Plitt Southern Theatres, Inc. Employees Fund
1801 Century Park East
Suite 1225
Los Angeles, CA 90067
phone: N/A

Description: Welfare assistance grants
Restrictions: Limited to employees of Plitt Southern Theatres
$ Given: Grants range from $199 - $10,068.
Application Information: Write for guidelines
Deadline: N/A
Contact: Joe S. Jackson, President

CORPORATE/EMPLOYEE GRANTS

· · · · · · · · · · · · · · · · · · · ·

CONNECTICUT

AMAX Aid Fund, Inc.
AMAX Center
Greenwich, CT 06836
phone: N/A

Description: Financial assistance to needy employees, former employees, and families of deceased employees of AMAX, Inc. and its subsidiaries
Restrictions: Individuals earning an annual salary from AMAX or receiving an AMAX pension are not eligible
$ Given: Four grants totaling $7,150 are awarded to individuals.
Application Information: Write for guidelines
Deadline: N/A
Contact: David George Ball, Senior Vice President

IDAHO

Morrison-Knudsen Employees Foundation, Inc.
One Morrison-Knudsen Plaza
Boise, ID 83729
(208) 386-5000

Description: Need-based assistance
Restrictions: Limited to employees of Morrison-Knudsen
$ Given: 24 grants totaling $114,200 are awarded to individuals; range, $700 - $8,900.
Application Information: Write or call for guidelines
Deadline: None
Contact: M.M. Puckett, Foundation Manager

ILLINOIS

The Clara Abbott Foundation
One Abbott Park Road
Abbott Park, IL 60064-3500
(312) 937-1091

Description: Relief grants and loans to employees and retired employees of Abbott Laboratories, as well as to members of their families. Aid to aged and indigent individuals
Restrictions: Limited to employees, retirees and families of employees of Abbott Laboratories
$ Given: 516 relief grants totaling $867,973 are awarded to individuals; 68 grants totaling $145,398 are awarded to the aged; range, $60 - $10,800.
Application Information: Write or call for guidelines
Deadline: None
Contact: David C. Jefferies, Executive Director

• • • • • • • • • • • • • • • • • • • •

Walgreen Benefit Fund
200 Wilmot Road
Deerfield, IL 60015
(708) 940-2931

Description: Welfare assistance grants
Restrictions: Limited to Walgreen employees and their families
$ Given: In FY90, an unspecified number of grants totaling $305,000 were awarded to individuals.
Application Information: Initial contact by letter
Deadline: None
Contact: Edward H. King, Vice President

MASSACHUSETTS

Charles F. Bacon Trust
c/o Bank of New England, N.A.
28 State Street
Boston, MA 02107
(617) 573-6416

Description: Assistance grants
Restrictions: Limited to former employees of Conrad and Chandler Company who have retired/resigned due to illness
$ Given: Six grants totaling $28,000 are awarded to individuals; range, $2,000 - $7,000.
Application Information: Initial contact by letter
Deadline: December 31
Contact: Kerry Herlilhy, Senior Vice President, Bank of New England

Henry Hornblower Fund, Inc.
Box 2365
Boston, MA 02169
(617) 589-3286

Description: Need-based grants
Restrictions: Limited to current and former employees of Hornblower & Weeks
$ Given: Two grants totaling $6,000 are awarded to individuals; range, $1,000 - $5,000.
Application Information: Initial contact by letter
Deadline: None
Contact: Nathan N. Withington, President

CORPORATE/EMPLOYEE GRANTS

. . . .

MICHIGAN

**Hudson-Webber
Foundation**
333 West Fort Street
Suite 1310
Detroit, MI 48226
(313) 963-7777

Description: Counseling services and last-resort financial assistance. Grants provided primarily in cases involving problems with physical or emotional health, and in financial emergencies
Restrictions: Limited to employees and qualified retired employees of the J.L. Hudson Company
$ Given: Grants range from $500 - $1,000.
Application Information: Formal application required for review by the foundation's trustees; interviews required
Deadline: None
Contact: Gilbert Hudson, President

MINNESOTA

CENEX Foundation
5500 Cenex Drive
Inver Grove Heights, MN
55075
(612) 451-5105

Description: Financial assistance grants
Restrictions: Limited to former employees of CENEX and its affiliates
$ Given: Grants range from $1,500 - $7,512.
Application Information: Initial contact by letter; formal application required
Deadline: None
Contact: N/A

MISSOURI

**Butler Manufacturing
Company Foundation**
Penn Valley Park
P.O. Box 419917
BMA Tower
Kansas City, MO 64141-
0197
(816) 968-3208

Description: Hardship grants to aid individuals in emergency financial distress due to serious illness, fire, or natural disaster
Restrictions: Limited to Butler Manufacturing Company employees, retirees and their dependents
$ Given: Three hardship grants totaling $10,650 are awarded; range, $650 - $8,000; general range, $500 - $2,000.
Application Information: Write for application guidelines and program information; interviews required
Deadline: None
Contact: Barbara Lee Fay, Foundation Administrator

• • • • • • • • • • • • • • • • • • •

Hall Family Foundations
c/o Charitable and Crown
Investment
Department 323
P.O. Box 419580
Kansas City, MO 64141-
6580
(816) 274-8516

Description: Grants for emergency relief assistance
Restrictions: Strictly limited to employees of Hallmark
$ Given: Total giving is $1,716,987; relief assistance
subtotal unspecified.
Application Information: Write or call for guidelines
Deadline: N/A
Contact: Margaret H. Pence, Director/Program Officer

**Kansas City Life Employ-
ees Welfare Fund**
3520 Broadway
Kansas City, MO 64111-
2565
(816) 753-7000

Description: Medical assistance grants
Restrictions: Limited to Kansas City Life employees and
their spouses and/or dependents
$ Given: Grants range from $950 - $3,313.
Application Information: Initial contact by letter
Deadline: None
Contact: Dennis M. Gaffney

**David May Employees
Trust Fund**
Sixth and Olive Streets
St. Louis, MO 63101
phone: N/A

Description: Need-based grants
Restrictions: Limited to employees and former employ-
ees of the May Department Stores Company
$ Given: An unspecified number of grants totaling
$11,500 are awarded to individuals.
Application Information: Write for guidelines
Deadline: N/A
Contact: N/A

**Edward F. Swinney
Foundation**
c/o Boatmen's First
National Bank of Kansas
City
P.O. Box 419038
Kansas City, MO 64183
(816) 234-7481

Description: Need-based grants
Restrictions: Limited to employees of Boatmen's First
National Bank of Kansas City
$ Given: Grants range from $9 - $5,621.
Application Information: Formal application required
Deadline: None
Contact: David P. Ross, Trust Officer

CORPORATE/EMPLOYEE GRANTS

• • • • • • • • • • • • • • • • • • •

NEVADA

George S. Ladd Memorial Fund
c/o V.M. Edwards
633 Folsom Street
Room 420
San Francisco, CA 94107
phone: N/A

Description: Financial assistance grants, including funding for medical treatment
Restrictions: Limited to elderly and retired employees of Pacific Bell, Nevada Bell and Pacific Northwest Bell
$ Given: Grants range from $1,271 - $4,450.
Application Information: Write for guidelines
Deadline: N/A
Contact: N/A

NEW JERSEY

Ittleson-Beaumont Fund
(formerly Ittleson Beneficial Fund)
c/o The C.I.T. Group Holdings, Inc.
135 West 50th Street
New York, NY 10020
(212) 408-6000
APPLICATION ADDRESS:
650 CIT Drive, Livingston, NJ 07039

Description: Need-based grants to provide supplemental income to individuals demonstrating continuing financial hardship
Restrictions: Intended primarily, but not exclusively, for current and former employees of C.I.T. Financial Corporation and its affiliates, as well as for the families of employees
$ Given: Grants range from $285 - $18,000.
Application Information: Submit application letter stating reason for request and providing details of applicant's financial status
Deadline: None
Contact: Clare Carmichael

NEW YORK

Cesare Barbieri Dixie Cup Employees Foundation
c/o Bankers Trust Company
P.O. Box 829
Church Street Station
New York, NY 10008
APPLICATION ADDRESS:
280 Park Avenue, New York, NY 10017
(212) 850-2291

Description: Grants to Dixie Cup Company employees and their beneficiaries, to provide tax-exempt benefits
Restrictions: Limited to employees of Dixie Cup Company and their beneficiaries
$ Given: Grants range from $14 - $585.
Application Information: Write or call for guidelines
Deadline: N/A
Contact: Margery Finnin, Trust Officer

• •

Richard D. Brown Trust B
c/o Chemical Bank
Administrative Services
Department
30 Rockefeller Plaza
New York, NY 10112
(212) 621-2143

Description: Need-based loans
Restrictions: Limited to employees of Chemical Bank
$ Given: An unspecified number of loans to individuals totaling $10,722 are made.
Application Information: Recipients chosen by staff benefits committee
Deadline: None
Contact: Mrs. B. Strohmeier

The Ernst & Young Foundation
(formerly The Ernst & Whinney Foundation)
277 Park Avenue
New York, NY 10172
phone: N/A

Description: Financial assistance grants to employees and their families
Restrictions: Limited to Ernst & Young employees and their families
$ Given: One relief grant for $2,400 is awarded.
Application Information: Write for guidelines
Deadline: N/A
Contact: Bruce J. Mantia, Administrator

Ittleson-Beaumont Fund
(formerly Ittleson Beneficial Fund)
c/o The C.I.T. Group
Holdings, Inc.
135 West 50th Street
New York, NY 10020
(212) 408-6000
APPLICATION ADDRESS:
650 CIT Drive, Livingston, NJ 07039

Description: Need-based grants to provide supplemental income to individuals demonstrating continuing financial hardship
Restrictions: Intended primarily, but not exclusively, for current and former employees of C.I.T. Financial Corporation and its affiliates, as well as for the families of employees
$ Given: Grants range from $285 - $18,000.
Application Information: Submit application letter stating reason for request and providing details of applicant's financial status
Deadline: None
Contact: Clare Carmichael

CORPORATE/EMPLOYEE GRANTS

• •

Glenn L. Martin Foundation
c/o Fiduciary Trust Company of New York
Two World Trade Center
New York, NY 10048
(212) 466-4100

Description: Welfare assistance grants
Restrictions: Limited to retired employees of the Martin Marietta Corporation
$ Given: Grants range from $100 - $2,500.
Application Information: Write or call for guidelines
Deadline: N/A
Contact: N/A

McCrory Corporation Needy & Worthy Employees Trust
c/o Chase Manhattan Bank, N.A.
Tax Services Division
1211 Avenue of the Americas
36th Floor
New York, NY 10036
phone: N/A

Description: Need-based grants
Restrictions: Limited to worthy employees of the McCrory Corporation
$ Given: Grants range from $5,000 - $7,444.
Application Information: Write for guidelines
Deadline: N/A
Contact: Larry Tynan

United Merchants & Manufacturers Employees Welfare Foundation
1407 Broadway
6th Floor
New York, NY 10018-5103
phone: N/A

Description: Need-based grants
Restrictions: Limited to current and former employees of United Merchants & Manufacturers, Inc., and to members of their families
$ Given: Grants range from $375 - $825.
Application Information: Write for guidelines
Deadline: None
Contact: Lawrence Marx, Jr., Trustee

NORTH CAROLINA

**Burlington Industries
Foundation**
P.O. Box 21207
3330 West Friendly Avenue
Greensboro, NC 27420
(919) 379-2515

Description: Emergency grants designed to aid individuals who have experienced severe loss from disaster
Restrictions: Limited to Burlington Industries employees and their families; primary focus of giving in North Carolina, South Carolina and Virginia
$ Given: Grants range from $250 - $1,000.
Application Information: Call or write for program information; interviews upon request
Deadline: None
Contact: Park R. Davidson, Executive Director

OHIO

**National Machinery
Foundation, Inc.**
Greenfield Street
P.O. Box 747
Tiffin, OH 44883
(419) 447-5211

Description: Need-based grants
Restrictions: Limited to former employees of National Machinery and to other financially distressed individuals in Seneca County, Ohio
$ Given: 205 relief grants totaling $69,950 are awarded to individuals; range, $150 - $4,000.
Application Information: Initial contact by letter
Deadline: N/A
Contact: D.B. Bero, Administrator

**Richman Brothers
Foundation**
Box 657
Chagrin Falls, OH 44022
(216) 247-5426

Description: Relief assistance grants
Restrictions: Limited to employees, pensioners, widows, and children of employees of the Richman Brothers Company; preference to individuals in Cleveland, Ohio
$ Given: Grants range from $100 - $1,995.
Application Information: Write for guidelines; formal application required
Deadline: November 15
Contact: Richard R. Moore, President

CORPORATE/EMPLOYEE GRANTS

• •

OREGON

**Journal Publishing
Company Employees
Welfare Fund, Inc.**
P.O. Box 3168
Portland, OR 97208
phone: N/A

Description: Welfare assistance grants
Restrictions: Limited to employees of Journal Publishing
Company
$ Given: Grants range from $1,200 - $3,600.
Application Information: Write for guidelines
Deadline: None
Contact: N/A

**George S. Ladd Memorial
Fund**
c/o V.M. Edwards
633 Folsom Street
Room 420
San Francisco, CA 94107
phone: N/A

Description: Financial assistance grants, including
funding for medical treatment
Restrictions: Limited to elderly and retired employees of
Pacific Bell, Nevada Bell and Pacific Northwest Bell
$ Given: Grants range from $1,271 - $4,450.
Application Information: Write for guidelines
Deadline: N/A
Contact: N/A

PENNSYLVANIA

**Vang Memorial
Foundation**
P.O. Box 11727
Pittsburgh, PA 15228
(412) 563-0261

Description: Grants-in-aid
Restrictions: Limited to past, present and future
employees of George Vang, Inc. and related companies,
and their dependents
$ Given: 15 grants totaling $29,233 are awarded to
individuals; range, $670 - $5,251; general range, $720 -
$2,000.
Application Information: Submit introductory letter,
including name, address and telephone number of
applicant and specifying type of grant requested and
basis of need
Deadline: None
Contact: E.J. Hosko, Treasurer

• • • • • • • • • • • • • • • • • • • •

SOUTH CAROLINA

Burlington Industries Foundation
P.O. Box 21207
3330 West Friendly Avenue
Greensboro, NC 27420
(919) 379-2515

Description: Emergency grants designed to aid individuals who have experienced severe loss from disaster
Restrictions: Limited to Burlington Industries employees and their families; primary focus of giving in North Carolina, South Carolina and Virginia
$ Given: Grants range from $250 - $1,000.
Application Information: Call or write for program information; interviews upon request
Deadline: None
Contact: Park R. Davidson, Executive Director

TEXAS

Amon G. Carter Star Telegram Employees Fund
P.O. Box 17480
Fort Worth, TX 76102
(817) 332-3535

Description: Medical/hardship assistance and pension supplements
Restrictions: Limited to employees of the Fort Worth Star-Telegram, KXAS-TV, and WBAP-Radio
$ Given: 28 welfare assistance grants totaling $233,017 are awarded; range, $844 - $7,964.
Application Information: Initial contact by letter
Deadline: None
Contact: Nenetta Tatum, President

The Mary L. Peyton Foundation
Bassett Tower
Suite 908
303 Texas Avenue
El Paso, TX 79901
(915) 533-9698

Description: Need-based grants to provide medical attention, food, and other necessities to those unable to meet these needs for themselves. Designed for those who have no other resources and who cannot obtain funds elsewhere.
Restrictions: Limited to legal residents/citizens of El Paso County, Texas; preference to children of needy current or former employees of Peyton Packing Company
$ Given: Grants range from $8 - $1,600
Application Information: Write for informational brochure; submit letter explaining economic situation and including itemization of basic services for which funding is requested
Deadline: None
Contact: James Day, Executive Director

CORPORATE/EMPLOYEE GRANTS

• •

VIRGINIA

Burlington Industries Foundation
P.O. Box 21207
3330 West Friendly Avenue
Greensboro, NC 27420
(919) 379-2515

Description: Emergency grants designed to aid individuals who have experienced severe loss from disaster
Restrictions: Limited to Burlington Industries employees and their families; primary focus of giving in North Carolina, South Carolina and Virginia
$ Given: Grants range from $250 - $1,000.
Application Information: Call or write for program information; interviews upon request
Deadline: None
Contact: Park R. Davidson, Executive Director

WASHINGTON

George S. Ladd Memorial Fund
c/o V.M. Edwards
633 Folsom Street
Room 420
San Francisco, CA 94107
phone: N/A

Description: Financial assistance grants, including funding for medical treatment
Restrictions: Limited to elderly and retired employees of Pacific Bell, Nevada Bell and Pacific Northwest Bell
$ Given: Grants range from $1,271 - $4,450.
Application Information: Write for guidelines
Deadline: N/A
Contact: N/A

• • • • • • • • • • • • • • • • • • •

COMPANIES WITH EMPLOYEES NATIONWIDE AND ABROAD

The Correspondents Fund
c/o Rosenman & Cohen
575 Madison Avenue
New York, NY 10022-2511
phone: N/A
APPLICATION ADDRESS: c/o The New York Times, 229 West 43rd Street, New York, NY 10036

Description: Emergency grants
Restrictions: Limited to individuals who have worked in the U.S. press, television, radio, news, film, and other U.S. organizations within or outside the U.S., and to individuals who have worked in the foreign press or other foreign news organizations, and to their dependents
$ Given: Grants range from $2,500 - $3,000.
Application Information: Submit an introductory letter, including details of the circumstances for which aid is requested
Deadline: None
Contact: James L. Greenfield, President

The Crane Fund
202 West Adams Street
Room 849
Chicago, IL 60606
phone: N/A

Description: Need-based grants
Restrictions: Open to former employees of Crane Company in the U.S. and Great Britain
$ Given: 1,366 grants totaling $1,646,392 are awarded to individuals.
Application Information: Write for guidelines
Deadline: None
Contact: Fern N. Brodie, Senior Caseworker

Roger L. Von Amelunxen Foundation, Inc.
83-21 Edgerton Boulevard
Jamaica, NY 11432
(718) 641-4800

Description: Welfare assistance grants
Restrictions: Limited to financially distressed families of U.S. Customs Service employees
$ Given: Nine welfare assistance grants totaling $21,000 are awarded to individuals; range, $500 - $5,000.
Application Information: Submit letter with proof of relationship to U.S. Customs Service employee
Deadline: August 1
Contact: Karen Donnelly, Vice President

Flow-through Funding

Many foundations will give monies to individuals indirectly; that is, individuals must apply under the auspices of nonprofit organizations. Grants are paid directly to medical institutions or organizations for the benefit of individuals in financial need. The nonprofit organization acts as the individual's sponsor or parent organization. The monies awarded are paid directly to the nonprofit organization, which passes them along to the individual. This is known as *flow-through* funding. Usually the nonprofit organization receives a fee of three to seven percent (3% - 7%) of monies raised. There is *no* up-front fee paid to the sponsor/parent organization. The three to seven percent fee is customary; it is not an obligation.

How do you go about finding a nonprofit conduit? Check any local directory of nonprofit organizations (your local library will usually have such directories in its collection, perhaps in a community services section). Contact local citywide consortium-styled associations operating in your area of interest, such as the United Way, health planning bodies, federations, and so on. Speak to their directors or public information officers and elicit their suggestions for possible sponsors. Also check national organizational reference books, such as the *Encyclopedia of Associations*, for other potential candidates.

FLOW-THROUGH FUNDING

. . . .

ALABAMA

The Greater Birmingham Foundation
P.O. Box 131027
Birmingham, AL 32513
(205) 933-0753

Description: Promotes the health, welfare, cultural, educational, and social needs of the Birmingham area
$ Given: $1,505,875 for grants
Application: Initial approach by letter
Deadline: None
Contact: Mrs. William McDonald, Jr., Executive Director

Child Health Foundation
P.O. Box 530964
Birmingham, AL 35253
(205) 251-9966

Description: The foundation's objective is to reduce illness and disease in children
$ Given: $66,654 in group grants; range, $5,103-$31,200, and $50,250 in grants to individuals
Application: Initial approach by letter
Deadline: August 31
Contact: Dr. Sergio Stagno, Executive Director

Hargis (Estes H. and Florence Parker) Charitable Foundation
317 20th Street North
P.O. Box 370404
Birmingham, AL 35237
(205) 251-2881

Description: Funding for health and youth services
$ Given: Seven grants totaling $395,374; range, $300-$376,075
Areas of Support: Alabama, Tennessee
Application: Initial approach by letter
Deadline: May 1
Contact: Gerald D. Colvin, Jr., Chair

D.W. McMillan Foundation
329 Belleville Avenue
P.O. Box 867
Brewton, AL 36427
(205) 867-4881

Description: Funds local health and welfare organizations (limited to programs giving direct aid)
$ Given: 21 grants totaling $392,000; range, $1,500-$60,000
Areas of Support: Escambia County, Alabama, and Escambia County, Florida
Application: Initial approach by letter
Deadline: December 1
Contact: James D. Nabors, Secretary-Treasurer

• •

Monsanto Fund
800 North Lindbergh
Boulevard
St. Louis, MO 63167
(314) 694-4596

Description: Funding interests include health services, hospitals, social services, youth, education (science and mathematics), and community funds
$ Given: Grants totaling $8,285,748; range, $100-$1,112,000
Areas of Support: Alabama, California, Florida, Georgia, Idaho, Illinois, Massachusetts, Maine, Missouri, New Jersey, North Carolina, Ohio, South Carolina, Texas, and West Virginia
Application: Proposal
Deadline: None
Contact: John L. Mason, President

ALASKA

Meyer Memorial Trust
1515 S.W. Fifth Avenue
Suite 500
Portland, OR 97201
(503) 228-5512

Description: General purpose grants for education, health and social welfare, arts and humanities; special program grants for Aging and Independence and Support for Children at Risk in Oregon, Alaska, Idaho, Montana, and Washington; operates a Small Grants Program ($500-$8,000) for small projects in Oregon
$ Given: 209 grants totaling $11,953,746; range, $500-$2,000,000
Application: Application form required
Deadline: April 1, October 1 for Aging and Independence; July 15, October 15 for Small Grants Program; no deadline for general purpose grants
Contact: Charles S. Rooks, Executive Director

ARIZONA

Arizona Community Foundation
4350 East Camelback Road
Suite 216 C
Phoenix, AZ 85018
(602) 952-9954

Description: Funds children's mental health, youth agencies, health agencies, organizations for the handicapped, and other human services programs
$ Given: 182 grants totaling $2,017,865; average range, $1,000-$10,000
Application: Initial approach by letter or telephone
Deadlines: February 1, June 1, October 1
Contact: Steven D. Mittenthal, President

FLOW-THROUGH FUNDING

. . . .

FHP Foundation
401 East Ocean Boulevard
Suite 206
Long Beach, CA 90802
(310) 590-8655

Description: Funds direct delivery of health care services, including education programs, programs for the elderly and chronically ill, and primary care projects in underserved areas.
$ Given: 17 grants totaling $773,064; range, $2,900-$89,000
Areas of Support: Giving in southern California, Utah, New Mexico, and Arizona
Application: Initial approach by letter
Deadline: February 15, May 15, August 15, and November 15
Contact: Sandra Lund Gavin, Executive Director

ARKANSAS

Arkansas Community Foundation, Inc.
604 East 6th Street
Little Rock, AR 72202
(501) 372-1116

Description: Areas of support include health, community development, social services, and education
$ Given: Grants totaling $958,642
Application: Initial approach by letter or telephone
Deadlines: January 1, April 1, September 1, and October 1
Contact: Martha Ann Jones, Executive Director

Arkla Corporate Giving Program
400 East Capitol Avenue
P.O. Box 751
Little Rock, AR 72203
(501) 377-4610

Description: Funds a wide variety of programs, including health services, mental health, AIDS, child welfare and drug abuse.
$ Given: N/A
Limitations: Giving in major operating areas (Arkansas, California, Kansas, Texas, Oklahoma, and Mississippi)
Application: Initial approach by letter
Deadline: None
Contact: James L. Rutherford III, Senior Vice President (Little Rock, Arkansas area) or Hugh H. McCastlain (Shreveport, Louisiana area)

The Walton (Sam M. and Helen R.) Foundation
125 West Central
No. 210
Bentonville, Arkansas 72712
(501) 273-5743

Description: Funds health services, education, youth programs, social services, and religious support
$ Given: Grants totaling $440,633; high, $100,000
Application: Initial approach by letter or telephone
Deadline: None
Contact: Jan Ney

CALIFORNIA

The Annenberg Fund, Inc.
St. Davids Center
150 Radnor Chester Road
Suite A 200
St. Davids, PA 19087
(215) 341-9270

Description: Funding interests include education, health and medical research, community service, and cultural programs
$ Given: 150 grants totaling $6,020,616; range, $100-$1,666,667
Areas of Support: Pennsylvania, California, New York
Application: Applications not accepted; giving to pre-selected organizations
Deadline: N/A
Contact: Alice C. Cory, Secretary-Treasurer

Argyros Foundation
950 South Coast Drive
Suite 200
Costa Mesa, CA 92626
(714) 241-5000

Description: Funds education, religious giving, social services, recreation, and health services
$ Given: 90 grants totaling $915,000; range, $50-$145,000
Application: Proposal
Deadline: June 1
Contact: Chuck Packard, Trustee

Arkla Corporate Giving Program
400 East Capitol Avenue
P.O. Box 751
Little Rock, AK 72203
(501) 377-4610

Description: Funds a wide variety of programs, including health services, mental health, AIDS, child welfare and drug abuse.
$ Given: N/A
Limitations: Giving in major operating areas (Arkansas, California, Kansas, Texas, Oklahoma, and Mississippi)
Application: Initial approach by letter
Deadline: None
Contact: James L. Rutherford III, Senior Vice President (Little Rock, Arkansas area) or Hugh H. McCastlain (Shreveport, Louisiana area)

The Bialis Family Foundation
c/o Melveny and Meyers
1800 Century Park East
Suite 600
Los Angeles, CA 90067
(213) 553-6700

Description: Funds social services, education, health services, and Jewish organizations
$ Given: 38 grants totaling $204,373; range, $500-$15,000
Application: Applications not accepted; giving to pre-selected organizations
Deadline: N/A
Contact: N/A

FLOW-THROUGH FUNDING

. . . .

Community Foundation of Santa Clara County
960 West Hedding
No. 220
San Jose, CA 95126
(408) 241-2666

Description: Funding includes health and social services
$ Given: 300 grants totaling $1,471,969; average range, $2,500-$15,000
Application: Initial approach by letter
Deadline: N/A
Contact: Peter Hero, Executive Director

The Mary A. Crocker Trust
233 Post Street
Second Floor
San Francisco, CA 94108
(415) 982-0139

Description: Funds child welfare, social services, women's projects, education, health services, and community development
$ Given: 48 grants totaling $490,080; range, $3,000-$50,000
Application: Initial approach by letter
Deadline: None
Contact: Barbaree Jernigan, Administrator

Freeman E. Fairfield Foundation
3610 Long Beach Boulevard
P.O. Box 7798
Long Beach, CA 90807
(310) 427-7219

Description: Supports youth agencies, medical centers and clinics, handicapped and general social services, including the aged and child welfare and development
$ Given: 20 grants totaling $378,486; average range, $5,000-$20,000
Application: Initial approach by letter
Deadline: May 1
Contact: Edna E. Sellers, Trustee

Fannie Mae Foundation
3900 Wisconsin Avenue NW
Washington, DC 20016
(202) 752-6500

Description: Funding interests include housing and community development, and health and social concerns
$ Given: 300 grants totaling $1,151,567; range, $100-$50,000
Areas of Support: Washington, DC; Pasadena, California; Atlanta, Georgia; Chicago, Illinois; and Philadelphia, Pennsylvania
Application: Proposal
Deadline: None
Contact: Harriet M. Ivey, Executive Director

• •

The Favrot Fund
909 Wirt Road
No. 101
Houston, TX 77024
(713) 956-4009

Description: Focus on community-based programs directed toward health, the needy, and the arts
$ Given: 24 grants totaling $310,000; range, $2,000-$25,000
Areas of Support: Texas, California, New York, and Washington, DC
Application: Initial approach by letter
Deadline: None
Contact: Mrs. Carol Parker

FHP Foundation
401 East Ocean Boulevard
Suite 206
Long Beach, CA 90802
(310) 590-8655

Description: Funds direct delivery of health care services, including education programs, programs for the elderly and chronically ill, and primary care projects in underserved areas.
$ Given: 17 grants totaling $773,064; range, $2,900-$89,000
Areas of Support: Giving in southern California, Utah, New Mexico, and Arizona
Application: Initial approach by letter
Deadline: February 15, May 15, August 15, and November 15
Contact: Sandra Lund Gavin, Executive Director

**First Nationwide Bank
Corporate Giving Program**
700 Market Street
San Francisco, CA 94102
(415) 772-1575

Description: Funds community, social, and health services
$ Given: 220 grants totaling $305,000; range, $150-$20,000
Application: Application form not required; write for guidelines
Deadline: None
Contact: Stephen L. Johnson, Senior Vice President

**The Garland (John Jewett
and H. Chandler)
Foundation**
P.O. Box 550
Pasadena, CA 91102

Description: Funds social services for the elderly, youth agencies, hospitals and health services
$ Given: 50 grants totaling $1,261,500; average range, $5,000-$20,000
Application: Initial approach by letter
Deadline: None
Contact: N/A

FLOW-THROUGH FUNDING

• •

The Fred Gellert Foundation
1655 Southgate Avenue
Suite 203
Daly City, CA 94015
(415) 991-1855

Description: Funds cultural programs, hospitals, health care programs, programs for the disabled, and social service agencies
$ Given: 95 grants totaling $649,733; range, $300-$100,000
Areas of Support: Giving in San Francisco and San Mateo counties, California
Application: Initial approach by letter
Deadline: None
Contact: Fred Gellert, Jr., Chairman

The William G. Gilmore Foundation
120 Montgomery Street
Suite 1880
San Francisco, CA 94104
(415) 546-1400

Description: Funds community-based organization, including family and social services, health services, and AIDS programs
$ Given: 132 grants totaling $766,345; range, $200-$50,000
Areas of Support: Giving in northern California, Oregon, and Washington
Application: Initial approach by letter
Deadlines: May 1, November 1
Contact: Faye Wilson, Secretary

Great American Corporate Giving Program
600 B Street
Suite 800
San Diego, CA 92101
(619) 231-6242

Description: Funds community health care, education, and the arts
$ Given: N/A
Application: Initial approach by letter
Deadline: None
Contact: Karen Miller, Community Relations Officer

Hedco Foundation
c/o Fitzgerald, Abbott and Beardsley
1221 Broadway
21st Floor
Oakland, CA 94612

Description: Funds educational and health service institutions
$ Given: 23 grants totaling $1,019,454; range, $500-$469,160
Application: Proposal
Deadline: None
Contact: Mary A. Goriup, Foundation Manager

• • • • • • • • • • • • • • • • • • • •

The James Irvine Foundation
One Market Plaza
Spear Tower
Suite 1715
San Francisco, CA 94105
(415) 644-1362

Description: Funds private higher education, health associations and services, including AIDS programs
$ Given: 273 grants totaling $20,487,000; average range, $25,000-$750,000
Application: Initial approach by letter
Deadline: None
Contact: Luz A. Vega, Director of Grants Program

Irvine Health Foundation
4199 Campus Drive
Suite 550
Irvine, CA 92715
(714) 854-6484

Description: Funds community health care; supports research on health care systems and programs, health programs and clinics (including a senior care center and drug abuse programs)
$ Given: 10 grants totaling $913,441; range, $2,500-$300,000
Areas of Support: Orange County, California
Application: Initial approach by letter
Deadline: None
Contact: Edward B. Kaie, Executive Director

Jerome Foundation
2660 West Woodland Drive
Suite 160
Anaheim, CA 92801
(714) 995-1696

Description: Funds medical research, services for handicapped children and the blind, and hospitals and health services
$ Given: 17 grants totaling $147,383; range, $100-$124,534
Application: Form not required
Deadline: None
Contact: Pat Perry

George Frederick Jewett Foundation
One Maritime Plaza
Suite 990
San Francisco, CA 94111
(415) 421-1351

Description: Interests include health care and medical research and services
$ Given: 134 grants totaling $953,597; range, $500-$25,000
Areas of Support: San Francisco, California; eastern Washington; northern Idaho
Application: Initial approach by letter
Deadlines: February 15, May 15, August 15, and Nov. 1
Contact: Theresa A. Mullen, Program Director

FLOW-THROUGH FUNDING

• • • • • • • • • • • • • • • • • • • •

Livingston Memorial Foundation
625 North A Street
Oxnard, CA 93030
(805) 983-0561

Description: Funding support for health and health-related activites
$ Given: 27 grants totaling $313,750; range, $840-$165,000
Areas of Support: Ventura County, California
Application: Initial approach by letter
Deadline: February 1
Contact: Laura K. McAvoy

Bert William Martin Foundation
c/o The Northern Trust Company
50 South LaSalle Street
Chicago, Illinois 60675
(312) 630-6000

Description: Funds hospitals and health services
$ Given: 23 grants totaling $147,700; range, $300-$75,000
Areas of Support: California and Mount Vernon, Ohio
Application: Applications not accepted; giving to pre-selected organizations
Deadline: N/A
Contact: N/A

The Milken Family Foundation
c/o Foundations of the Milken Families
15250 Ventura Boulevard
Second Floor
Sherman Oaks, CA 91403

Description: Interests include health care and medical research, and to make the benefits of both basic and highly advanced health care available to those who need them
$ Given: Grants totaling $4,015,074; range, $100-$500,000
Application: Applications not accepted; giving to pre-selected organizations
Deadline: N/A
Contact: Dr. Jules Lesner, Executive Director

The Milken Family Medical Foundation
c/o Foundations of the Milken Families
15250 Ventura Boulevard
Second Floor
Sherman Oaks, CA 91403

Description: Interests include health care and medical research, and to make the benefits of both basic and highly advanced health care available to those who need them
$ Given: 68 grants totaling $4,524,310; range, $180-$950,000
Application: Applications not accepted; giving to pre-selected organizations
Deadline: N/A
Contact: Lori Milken, President

• •

Monsanto Fund
800 North Lindbergh
Boulevard
St. Louis, Missouri 63167
(314) 694-4596

Description: Funding interests include health services, hospitals, social services, youth, education (science and mathematics), and community funds
$ Given: Grants totaling $8,285,748; range, $100-$1,112,000
Areas of Support: Alabama, California, Florida, Georgia, Idaho, Illinois, Massachusetts, Maine, Missouri, New Jersey, North Carolina, Ohio, South Carolina, Texas, and West Virginia
Application: Proposal
Deadline: None
Contact: John L. Mason, President

The Norris (Kenneth T. and Eileen L.) Foundation
11 Golden Shore
Suite 440
Long Beach, CA 90802
(310) 435-8444

Description: Funds hospitals, health services, medical research, and social services
$ Given: 121 grants totaling $3,286,800; range, $1,000-$625,000
Application: Initial approach by letter
Deadline: None
Contact: Ronald R. Barnes, Executive Director

Mary Pickford Foundation
9171 Wilshire Boulevard
Suite 512
Beverly, Hills, CA 90210
(310) 273-2770

Description: Funds "well-established medical or community service organizations"
$ Given: 93 grants totaling $563,910; range, $135-$70,000
Application: Initial approach by letter
Deadline: None
Contact: Edward C. Stotsenberg, President

Santa Barbara Foundation
15 East Carillo Street
Santa Barbara, CA 93101
(805) 963-1873

Description: Funding includes social services, youth and health services
$ Given: 137 grants totaling $1,692,087
Application: N/A
Deadline: N/A
Contact: Edward R. Spaulding, Executive Director

FLOW-THROUGH FUNDING

The Sierra Foundation
12111 Gold Country
Boulevard
Suite 101
Rancho Cordova, CA 95670
(916) 635-4745

Description: Funds health-related programs that will have a long-term impact on the general health of the population, will provide a positive change in health care systems or in the use of health care resources
$ Given: 64 grants totaling $1,592,162; average range, $20,000-$40,000
Application: Initial approach by letter
Deadline: None
Contact: Len McCandliss, President

Swig Foundation
c/o The Swig Foundations
Fairmont Hotel
San Francisco, CA 94016
(415) 772-5375

Description: Funding for arts, culture, education, community welfare, medical care, and projects in Israel
$ Given: 197 grants totaling $1,230,960; average range, $1,000-$65,000
Application: Initial approach by letter
Deadline: None
Contact: Nat Starr, Director

Sally B. Thornton Foundation
2125 Evergreen Street
San Diego, CA 92106

Description: Funds cultural programs, education, and health services
$ Given: 66 grants totaling $432,684; range, $10-$190,000
Application: Applications not accepted; giving to pre-selected organizations
Deadline: N/A
Contact: N/A

Van Nuys (I.N. and Susanna H.) Foundation
c/o Security Pacific
National Bank
P.O. Box 3189
Terminal Annex
Los Angeles, CA 90051

Description: Grants for health services and education
$ Given: 17 grants totaling $633,827; range, $4,000-$333,200
Application: Initial approach by letter
Deadline: None
Contact: Lorraine Tessier, Accountant

• • • • • • • • • • • • • • • • • • • •

Van Nuys (J.B. and Emily) Charities
1800 Avenue of the Stars
Suite 345
Los Angeles, CA 90067
(213) 552-0175

Description: Funds hospitals and health service agencies, as well as child welfare and youth agencies
$ Given: 130 grants totaling $643,245; average, $5,000
Application: Proposal
Deadline: None
Contact: Robert Gibson Johnson, President

Wood-Claeyssens Foundation
P.O. Box 30547
Santa Barbara, CA 93130
(805) 682-4775

Description: Funds hospitals, health services, social services, and youth agencies
$ Given: 52 grants totaling $298,000; range, $500-$50,000
Application: Initial approach by letter
Deadline: August 31
Contact: Pierre V. Claeyssens, First Vice President

COLORADO

The Anschutz Family Foundation
2400 Anaconda Tower
555 17th Street
Denver, CO 80202
(303) 293-2338

Description: Funds direct human services, especially for children, the elderly, and the poor, including health services
$ Given: 140 grants totaling $606,900; range, $100-$55,000
Application: Initial approach by letter
Deadline: March 1, September 1
Contact: Sue Anschutz Rodgers, President

Comprecare Foundation, Inc.
P.O. Box 44170
Aurora, CO 80044
(303) 322-1641

Description: "To encourage, aid or assist specific health related programs and to support the activities of organizations and individuals who advance and promote health care education, the delivery of health care services, and the improvement of community health and welfare"
$ Given: 16 grants totaling $215,066; range, $2,000-$46,000
Application: Initial approach by letter
Deadline: None
Contact: N/A

FLOW-THROUGH FUNDING

. . . .

Gates Foundation
3200 Cherry Creek South
Drive
Suite 630
Denver, CO 80209
(303) 722-1881

Description: Funding interests include health care, health care cost reduction, and human services
$ Given: Grants totaling $3,911,887; high, $650,000
Application: Initial approach by telephone
Deadlines: January 15, April 15, July 15, and October 15
Contact: F. Charles Froelicher, Executive Director

Johnson (Helen K. and Arthur E.) Foundation
1700 Broadway
Room 2302
Denver, CO 80290
(303) 861-4127

Description: "To solve human problems and enrich the quality of human life"
$ Given: 111 grants totaling $2,897,029; range, $100-$250,000
Application: Initial approach by letter or proposal
Deadline: January 1, April 1, July 1, and September 1
Contact: Stan Kamprath, Executive Director

Keebler Company Foundation
One Hollow Tree Lane
Elmhurst, Illinois 60126
(312) 833-2900

Description: Funding interests include minority programs, health and human services, and education
$ Given: 239 grants totaling $359,987; range, $10-$34,180
Areas of Support: Illinois, Colorado, Indiana, Maine, Minnesota, North Carolina, Pennsylvania, Texas
Application: Initial approach by letter
Deadline: None
Contact: A.G. Bland, Treasurer

Stern-Elder Memorial Trust
1700 Broadway
Denver, CO 80274

Description: Funds performing arts, health organizations, and social services
$ Given: 52 grants totaling $271,250; range, $100-$50,000
Application: N/A
Deadline: N/A
Contact: N/A

CONNECTICUT

Louis H. Aborn Foundation, Inc.
46 Wilshire Road
Greenwich, CT 06830
(203) 661-4046

Description: Funds public health projects, education, and child welfare
$ Given: Four grants totaling $151,000; range, $1,000-$90,000
Application: Initial approach by letter
Deadline: None
Contact: Louis H. Aborn, President

Carolyn Foundation
1800 TCF Tower
Minneapolis, Minnesota 55402
(612) 339-7101

Description: Funding for health and welfare, education, culture, women, the environment, and the disadvantaged
$ Given: 37 grants totaling $989,665; range, $1,300-$100,000
Areas of Support: Minneapolis-St. Paul, Minnesota and New Haven, Connecticut
Application: Initial approach by letter
Deadline: January and February for grants under $10,000; January through July for grants over $10,000
Contact: Carol J. Fetzer, Executive Director

Crestlea Foundation, Inc.
1004 Wilmington Trust Court
Wilmington, DE 19801

Description: Funding emphasis includes health agencies, higher and secondary education, social services, and youth agencies
$ Given: 35 grants totaling $527,765; range, $500-$225,565
Areas of Support: Delaware and Connecticut
Application: Initial approach by letter
Deadline: None
Contact: Stewart E. Poole, President

Fairfield County Cooperative Foundation
Five Landmark Square
Stamford, CT 06901
(203) 323-7410

Description: Funds health and social services, arts and culture, and education
$ Given: 60 grants totaling $989,937; range, $1,000-$90,000
Application: Initial approach by letter requesting guidelines
Deadlines: One month prior to board meetings (board meets the third Friday in February, April, August, and October)
Contact: Betsy Rich, Executive Director

FLOW-THROUGH FUNDING

. . . .

Fisher Foundation, Inc.
36 Brookside Boulevard
West Hartford, CT 06107
(203) 523-7247

Description: Funds a Jewish welfare federation, health services, education, housing, the disadvantaged, and the aged
$ Given: 69 grants totaling $435,543; range, $100-$69,000
Application: Initial approach by letter
Deadlines: February 1, May 1, October 1
Contact: N/A

Hagedorn Fund
c/o Manufacturers Hanover
Trust Company
270 Park Avenue
New York, NY 10017
(212) 270-9107

Description: Funding for education, hospitals and health agencies, the aged, youth agencies, medical research, community funds, and cultural organizations
$ Given: 114 grants totaling $1,110,000; range, $1,000-$85,000
Areas of Support: New York metropolitan area (including New Jersey and Connecticut)
Application: Proposal
Deadline: November 15
Contact: Robert Rosenthal, Vice President, Manufacturers Hanover Trust Company

Heublein Foundation, Inc.
P.O. Box 388
Farmington, CT 06032
(203) 677-4061

Description: Funding interests include hospitals and health services
$ Given: 89 grants totaling $827,478; range, $500-$126,000
Application: Initial approach by letter
Deadline: N/A
Contact: L. Eileen Hall, Treasurer

The Howard and Bush Foundation, Inc.
85 Gillett Street
Hartford, CT 06105
(203) 236-8595

Description: Funding emphasis includes health services
$ Given: 77 grants totaling $1,346,985; range, $3,500-$72,052
Areas of Support: Hartford, Connecticut and Troy, New York
Application: Initial approach by letter
Deadline: February 1, June 1, October 1
Contact: Nancy Roberts

• • • • • • • • • • • • • • • • • • • •

The Travelers Companies Foundation
One Tower Square
Hanford, CT 06183
(203) 277-2307

Description: Funding interests include programs that benefit older Americans, and health and social services
$ Given: 171 grants totaling $4,043,833; range, $500-$835,000
Application: Proposal
Deadline: None
Contact: Janet C. French, Executive Director

The Waterbury Foundation
P.O. Box 252
Waterbury, CT 06720
(203) 753-1315

Description: Funds social services, health care, education, community funds, and the arts
$ Given: 45 grants totaling $269,946; range, $45-$100,000
Application: Initial approach by letter
Deadline: None
Contact: N/A

DELAWARE

Birch (Stephen and Mary) Foundation, Inc.
501 Silverside Road
Suite 13
Wilmington, DE 19809

Description: Funding emphasis includes health agencies, hospitals, social services, and youth agencies
$ Given: Eight grants totaling $1,695,500; range, $500-$1,500,000
Application: Initial approach by letter
Deadline: None
Contact: Elfriede Looze

Crestlea Foundation, Inc.
1004 Wilmington Trust Court
Wilmington, DE 19801

Description: Funding emphasis includes health agencies, higher and secondary education, social services, and youth agencies
$ Given: 35 grants totaling $527,765; range, $500-$225,565
Application: Initial approach by letter
Deadline: None
Contact: Stewart E. Poole, President

FLOW-THROUGH FUNDING

. . . .

Ederic Foundation, Inc.
Building C
Suite 300
3801 Kennett Pike
Greenville, DE 19807
(302) 654-9933

Description: Funding interests include hospitals and health care
$ Given: 94 grants totaling $329,805; range, $50-$38,000
Application: Initial approach by letter
Deadline: None
Contact: Harry S. Short, Secretary

DISTRICT OF COLUMBIA

Bender Foundation, Inc.
1120 Connecticut Avenue
NW
Suite 1200
Washington, DC 20036
(202) 828-9000

Description: Funding interests include education, health services, social welfare, Jewish organizations and welfare funds
$ Given: 65 grants totaling $395,200; range, $1,000-$100,000
Areas of Support: Washington, DC, and Maryland
Application: Initial approach by letter
Deadline: November 20
Contact: Sondra D. Bender, President

Fannie Mae Foundation
3900 Wisconsin Avenue,
N.W.
Washington, DC 20016
(202) 752-6500

Description: Funding interests include housing and community development, and health and social concerns
$ Given: 300 grants totaling $1,151,567; range, $100-$50,000
Areas of Support: Washington, DC; Pasadena, California; Atlanta, Georgia; Chicago, Illinois; and Philadelphia, Pennsylvania
Application: Proposal
Deadline: None
Contact: Harriet M. Ivey, Executive Director

The Favrot Fund
909 Wirt Road
No. 101
Houston, TX 77024
(713) 956-4009

Description: Focus on community-based programs directed toward health, the needy, and the arts
$ Given: 24 grants totaling $310,000; range, $2,000-$25,000
Areas of Support: Texas, California, New York, and Washington, DC
Application: Initial approach by letter
Deadline: None
Contact: Mrs. Carol Parker

Stewart (Alexander and Margaret) Trust
c/o First American Bank, N.A., Washington
740 15th Street, N.W.
Washington, DC 20005
(202) 637-7887

Description: Funding for the prevention of cancer and the care of those afflicted with cancer
$ Given: 15 grants totaling $993,559; range, $20,000-$175,000
Application: Applications not accepted; giving to pre-selected organizations
Deadline: N/A
Contact: N/A

FLORIDA

John Blair Foundation
c/o Northern Trust Bank of Florida/Naples, N.A.
530 Fifth Avenue South
Naples, FL 33940
(813) 262-8800

Description: Funds health and social services, and family planning.
$ Given: 48 grants totaling $105,600; range, $150-$15,000
Application: Application form not required
Deadline: None
Contact: N/A

Edyth Bush Charitable Foundation, Inc.
199 East Wellbourne Avenue
P.O. Box 1967
Winter Park, FL 32790
(407) 647-4322

Description: Funds charitable, educational, and health service organizations, with emphasis on human services and health
$ Given: 58 grants totaling $2,260,296; range, $4,000-$170,000
Application: Initial approach by letter or proposal
Deadlines: September 1, January 1
Contact: H. Clifford Lee, President

Conn Memorial Foundation, Inc.
220 East Madison Street
Suite 822
P.O. Box 229
Tampa, FL 33601
(813) 223-3838

Description: Funds health services and rehabilitation and charities benefitting youth
$ Given: 49 grants totaling $778,220; range, $1,000-$175,000
Application: Initial approach by letter or proposal
Deadline: November 30, May 31
Contact: David B. Frye, President

FLOW-THROUGH FUNDING

. . . .

**Dade Community
Foundation**
200 South Biscayne
Boulevard
Suite 4970
Miami, FL 33131
(305) 371-2711

Description: Funding interests include health, social services, the homeless and housing, education, arts and culture
$ Given: 305 grants totaling $1,601,360; range, $100-$62,140
Application: Initial approach by letter
Deadline: December 1
Contact: Ruth Shack, President

**James E. Davis Family -
W.D. Charities**
5050 Edgewood Court
Jacksonville, FL 32205

Description: Areas of support include education, medical research, and health services
$ Given: 19 grants totaling $130,650; range, $100-$50,000
Application: N/A
Deadline: N/A
Contact: N/A

**Tine W. Davis Family -
W.D. Charities, Inc.**
4190 Belfort Road
Suite 240
Jacksonville, FL 32216

Description: Areas of support include education, health and social service agencies, and medical research
$ Given: 117 grants totaling $762,425; range, $10,000-$100,000
Application: Initial approach by letter
Deadline: None
Contact: Charitable Grants Commission

**Jefferson Lee Ford III
Memorial Foundation, Inc.**
c/o Sun Bank Miami
9600 Collins Avenue
P.O. Box 546487
Bal Harbour, FL 33154
(305) 868-2630

Description: Funds health agencies, education, and medical research
$ Given: 48 grants totaling $198,500; range, $1,000-$15,000
Application: Initial approach by letter
Deadline: None
Contact: Herbert L. Kurras, Sr., Director

Charles A. Frueauff Foundation
306 East Seventh Avenue
Tallahassee, FL 32303
(904) 561-3508

Description: Areas of support include hospitals, mental health and other health services
$ Given: 195 grants totaling $2,824,500; range, $1,500-$50,000
Application: Initial approach by letter, telephone, or proposal
Deadline: March 15
Contact: David A. Frueauff, Secretary

K.W. Grader Foundation, Inc.
1925 Hermosa Street
Bartow, FL 33830
(813) 533-1048

Description: Funding for health services, higher education, religious giving, and social services, including child welfare
$ Given: 67 grants totaling $292,990; range, $250-$25,000
Application: Applications not accepted; giving to pre-selected organizations
Deadline: N/A
Contact: E.L. Grader, Vice President

Lost Tree Charitable Foundation, Inc.
11555 Lost Tree Way
North Palm Beach, FL 33408
(407) 622-3780

Description: Funding interests include education and health services
$ Given: 30 grants totaling $146,354; range, $500-$14,500
Application: Initial approach by letter
Deadline: None
Contact: Pamela M. Rue. Executive Secretary

D.W. McMillan Foundation
329 Belleville Avenue
P.O. Box 867
Brewton, AL 36427
(205) 867-4881

Description: Funds local health and welfare organizations (limited to programs giving direct aid)
$ Given: 21 grants totaling $392,000; range, $1,500-$60,000
Areas of Support: Escambia County, Alabama, and Escambia County, Florida
Application: Initial approach by letter
Deadline: December 1
Contact: James D. Nabors, Secretary-Treasurer

. . . .

Monsanto Fund
800 North Lindbergh
Boulevard
St. Louis, MO 63167
(314) 694-4596

Description: Funding interests include health services, hospitals, social services, youth, education (science and mathematics), and community funds
$ Given: Grants totaling $8,285,748; range, $100-$1,112,000
Areas of Support: Alabama, California, Florida, Georgia, Idaho, Illinois, Massachusetts, Maine, Missouri, New Jersey, North Carolina, Ohio, South Carolina, Texas, and West Virginia
Application: Proposal
Deadline: None
Contact: John L. Mason, President

Martha G. Moore
Foundation, Inc.
850 S.E. 7th Street
Suite A
Deerfield Beach, FL 33441

Description: Funds health and social services
$ Given: 13 grants totaling $125,000; range, $2,000-$28,000
Application: N/A
Deadline:N/A
Contact: N/A

Wilson (Hugh and Mary)
Foundation, Inc.
c/o Wood and Seitl
240 North Washington
Boulevard
Suite 460
Sarasota, FL 34236
(813) 954-2155

Description: Areas of support include cancer research and health services, the performing arts, and social service issues
$ Given: 26 grants totaling $238,291; range, $1,000-$50,000
Areas of Support: Manatee-Sarasota, Florida; Lewisburg-Danville, Pennsylvania
Application: Initial approach by letter
Deadline: None
Contact: John R. Wood, President

GEORGIA

Allen Foundation, Inc.
Box 1712
Atlanta, GA 30301
(404) 332-3000

Description: Funds education, health services, and cultural programs
$ Given: 73 grants totaling $289,066; range, $100-$47,400
Application: Application form required
Deadline: June 30
Contact: Roger E. Herndon, Secretary-Treasurer

• • • • • • • • • • • • • • • • • • • •

Fannie Mae Foundation
3900 Wisconsin Avenue NW
Washington, DC 20016
(202) 752-6500

Description: Funding interests include housing and community development, and health and social concerns
$ Given: 300 grants totaling $1,151,567; range, $100-$50,000
Areas of Support: Washington, DC; Pasadena, California; Atlanta, Georgia; Chicago, Illinois; and Philadelphia, PA
Application: Proposal
Deadline: None
Contact: Harriet M. Ivey, Executive Director

Fort Howard Foundation, Inc.
P.O. Box 11325
Green Bay, WI 54307
(414) 435-8821

Description: Areas of support include education, health care facilities, cultural programs, and social service and youth agencies
$ Given: 6 grants totaling $726,652; range, $13,700-$150,000
Areas of Support: Green Bay, Wisconsin; Muskogee, Oklahoma; and Effingham County, Georgia
Application: The foundation is not presently making any new funding commitments
Contact: Bruce W. Nagel, Executive Director

The Lee (Ray M. and Mary Elizabeth) Foundation, Inc.
c/o Citizens and Southern
Trust Company
P.O. Box 4446
Atlanta, GA 30302
(404) 897-3222

Description: Areas of support include health agencies, educational institutions, hospitals, religious organizations and the arts.
$ Given: 62 grants totaling $360,000; range, $1,000-$25,000
Application: Proposal
Deadlines: January 31, April 30, July 31, and October 31
Contact: Larry B. Hooks, Administrative Manager

Monsanto Fund
800 North Lindbergh
Boulevard
St. Louis, MO 63167
(314) 694-4596

Description: Funding interests include health services, hospitals, social services, youth, education (science and mathematics), and community funds
$ Given: Grants totaling $8,285,748; range, $100-$1,112,000
Areas of Support: Alabama, California, Florida, Georgia, Idaho, Illinois, Massachusetts, Maine, Missouri, New Jersey, North Carolina, Ohio, South Carolina, Texas, and West Virginia
Application: Proposal
Deadline: None
Contact: John L. Mason, President

FLOW-THROUGH FUNDING

• • • • • • • • • • • • • • • • • • • •

HAWAII

First Hawaiian Foundation
165 South King Street
Honolulu, HI 96813
(808) 525-8144

Description: Funds social services, health services, education, and a church and community fund
$ Given: 50 grants totaling $733,536; range, $177-$127,000
Application: Initial approach by letter
Deadline: None
Contact: Herbert E. Wolff, Secretary

Hawaiian Electric Industries Charitable Foundation
P.O. Box 730
Honolulu, HI 96808
(808) 543-7356

Description: Funding interests include health, hospitals, and community development
$ Given: 201 grants totaling $812,000; range, $300-$25,000
Application: Initial approach by letter with project data
Deadline: December 1, June 1
Contact: Ted Souza

IDAHO

George Frederick Jewett Foundation
One Maritime Plaza
Suite 990
San Franciso, CA 94111
(415) 421-1351

Description: Interests include health care and medical research and services
$ Given: 134 grants totaling $953,597; range, $500-$25,000
Areas of Support: San Francisco, California; eastern Washington; northern Idaho
Application: Initial approach by letter
Deadlines: February 15, May 15, August 15, and Nov. 1
Contact: Theresa A. Mullen, Program Director

Meyer Memorial Trust
1515 S.W. Fifth Avenue
Suite 500
Portland, OR 97201
(503) 228-5512

Description: General purpose grants in Oregon for education, health and social welfare, arts and humanities; special program grants for Aging and Independence and Support for Children at Risk in Oregon, Alaska, Idaho, Montana, and Washington; operates a Small Grants Program (500-$8,000) for small projects in Oregon
$ Given: 209 grants totaling $11,953,746; range, $500-$2,000,000
Application: Application form required
Deadline: April 1, October 1 for Aging and Independence; July 15, October 15 for Small Grants Program; no deadline for general purpose grants
Contact: Charles S. Rooks, Executive Director

Monsanto Fund
800 North Lindbergh
Boulevard
St. Louis, MO 63167
(314) 694-4596

Description: Funding interests include health services, hospitals, social services, youth, education (science and mathematics), and community funds
$ Given: Grants totaling $8,285,748; range, $100-$1,112,000
Areas of Support: Alabama, California, Florida, Georgia, Idaho, Illinois, Massachusetts, Maine, Missouri, New Jersey, North Carolina, Ohio, South Carolina, Texas, and West Virginia
Application: Proposal
Deadline: None
Contact: John L. Mason, President

Spokane Inland Northwest Community Foundation
400 Paulsen Center
West 421 Riverside Avenue
Spokane, Washington 99201
(509) 624-2606

Description: Funding interests include the elderly, music and the arts, social and health services, and education
$ Given: 440 grants totaling $738,429; average grant, $1,500
Areas of Support: The inland northwest (Washington and Idaho)
Application: Initial approach by letter
Deadlines: October 1 (Spokane, Washington); November 1 (Pullman and Dayton, Washington); May 1 (northern Idaho); and October 15 (ISC fund)
Contact: Jeanne L. Ager, Executive Director

ILLINOIS

The Blum (Nathan and Emily S.) Fund
c/o Harris Bank
111 West Monroe Street
P.O. Box 755
Chicago, IL 60690
(312) 461-2613

Description: Funds hospitals, health and social service agencies (including Jewish welfare funds)
$ Given: 10 grants totaling $360,000; range, $2,000-$102,000
Application: Proposal
Deadline: None
Contact: Ellen A. Bechtold, Vice President, Harris Trust and Savings Bank

Blum-Kovler Foundation
500 North Michigan Avenue
Chicago, IL 60611
(312) 828-9777

Description: Areas of support include education, hospitals, health services, and medical research
$ Given: 148 grants totaling $1,360,850; range, $500-$310,000
Application: Initial approach by letter
Deadline: None
Contact: H. Jonathan Kovler, Treasurer

FLOW-THROUGH FUNDING

• • • • • • • • • • • • • • • • • • • •

Borg-Warner Foundation, Inc.
200 South Michigan Avenue
Chicago, IL 60604
(312) 322-8659

Description: Funding interests include community funds, social welfare, and health services
$ Given: 150 grants totaling $1,295,445; range, $500-$200,000
Aplication: Initial approach by letter of intent
Deadline: March 1 (letter of intent); May 1 (proposal)
Contact: Ellen J. Benjamin, Director of Corporate Contributions

Fred J. Brunner Foundation
9300 King Street
Franklin Park, IL 60131

Description: Funds education, and social, health, and youth services.
$ Given: Grants totaling $221,540; range, $100-$20,000
Application: Proposal
Deadline: December 15
Contact: A.J. Schwegel, Vice President

A.C. Bueler Foundation
c/o Continental Illinois
National Bank and Trust
Colorado. of Chicago
30 North LaSalle Street
Chicago, IL 60693
(312) 828-1785

Description: Funds hospitals, health services, medical research, and education
$ Given: Five grants totaling $431,000
Application: Initial approach by letter
Deadline: None
Contact: M.C. Ryan

John Deere Foundation
John Deere Road
Moline, IL 61265
(309) 765-4137

Description: Areas of support include health services, community funds, youth agencies, and education
$ Given: Grants totaling $3,707,974; range, $300-$539,000
Areas of Support: Iowa, Illinois, Wisconsin
Application: Initial approach by letter
Deadline: None
Contact: Donald R. Morgenthaler, President

The Donaldson Foundation
c/o Donaldson Company, Inc.
P.O. Box 1299
Minneapolis, MN 55440
(612) 887-3010

Description: Funding interests include health services, environmental protection, and higher education
$ Given: 98 grants totaling $338,875; range, $300-$38,400
Areas of Support: Illinois, Indiana, Iowa, Kentucky, Minnesota, Missouri, and Wisconsin
Application: Initial approach by letter
Deadline: May 1, August 1
Contact: Raymond Vodovnik, Secretary

The Dumke (Dr. Ezekial R. and Edna Wattis) Foundation
600 Crandall Building
10 West First South
Salt Lake City, UT 84101
(801) 363-7863

Description: Funds education, medical and hospital services, youth agencies, and cultural programs
$ Given: 27 grants totaling $262,113; range, $1,000-$40,000
Areas of Support: Utah and Illinois
Application: Application form required
Deadline: February 1, July 1
Contact: Max B. Lewis, Secretary

Fannie Mae Foundation
3900 Wisconsin Avenue NW
Washington, DC 20016
(202) 752-6500

Description: Funding interests include housing and community development, and health and social concerns
$ Given: 300 grants totaling $1,151,567; range, $100-$50,000
Areas of Support: Washington, DC; Pasadena, California; Atlanta, Georgia; Chicago, Illinois; and Philadelphia, Pennsylvania
Application: Proposal
Deadline: None
Contact: Harriet M. Ivey, Executive Director

The Field Foundation of Illinois, Inc.
135 South LaSalle Street
Chicago, Il 60603
(312) 263-3211

Description: Funds health, community welfare, education, and cultural activities
$ Given: 57 grants totaling $1,579,109; range, $5,000-$97,000
Application: Proposal
Deadline: None
Contact: Handy L. Lindsey, Jr., Executive Director

FLOW-THROUGH FUNDING

• •

Lloyd A. Fry Foundation
135 South LaSalle Street
Suite 1910
Chicago, IL 60603
(312) 580-0310

Description: Areas of support include education, public policy, health and social services
$ Given: 153 grants totaling $2,651,460; range, $1,000-$115,000
Application: Initial approach by letter
Deadline: None
Contact: Ben Rothblatt, Executive Director

Iowa and Illinois Gas and Electric Company Giving Program
206 East Second Street
Davenport, IA 52802
(319) 326-7038

Description: Areas of support include education, health care, child welfare, civic affairs, community development, and family services
$ Given: 186 grants totaling $ 537,065; range, $10-$106,375
Areas of Support: Davenport, Bettendorf, Cedar Rapids, Iowa City, and Fort Dodge, Iowa; Rock Island and Moline, Illinois; and Ohio
Application: Initial approach by letter
Deadline: None
Contact: J.C. Decker, Secretary-Treasurer

Keebler Company Foundation
One Hollow Tree Lane
Elmhurst, IL 60126
(312) 833-2900

Description: Funding interests include minority programs, health and human services, and education
$ Given: 239 grants totaling $359,987; range, $10-$34,180
Areas of Support: Illinois, Colorado, Indiana, Maine, Minnesota, North Carolina, Pennsylvania, Texas
Application: Initial approach by letter
Deadline: None
Contact: A.G. Bland, Treasurer

Material Service Foundation
222 North LaSalle Street
Chicago, IL 60675

Description: Funding interests include health services, education, cultural activities, and community development
$ Given: 139 grants totaling $283,100; range, $25-$100,000
Application: Initial approach by letter
Deadline: None
Contact: Louis J. Levy, Administrator

Monsanto Fund
800 North Lindbergh
Boulevard
St. Louis, MO 63167
(314) 694-4596

Description: Funding interests include health services, hospitals, social services, youth, education (science and mathematics), and community funds
$ Given: Grants totaling $8,285,748; range, $100-$1,112,000
Areas of Support: Alabama, California, Florida, Georgia, Idaho, Illinois, Massachusetts, Maine, Missouri, New Jersey, North Carolina, Ohio, South Carolina, Texas, and West Virginia
Application: Proposal
Deadline: None
Contact: John L. Mason, President

Morton International Foundation
110 North Wacker Drive
Chicago, IL 60606

Description: Funds health and social services, education, civic affairs, and cultural programs
Given: 96 grants totaling $390,614; range, $500-$121,700
Application: Initial approach by letter
Deadline: None
Contact: N/A

The Northern Trust Company Charitable Trust
c/o The Northern Trust Company
50 South LaSalle Street
Chicago, IL 60675
(312) 444-3538

Description: Funds community development, health services, education, and social service
$ Given: 645 grants totaling $1,182,538; range, $25-$154,000
Application: Initial approach by letter or brief proposal
Deadline: Health: February 1
Contact: Marjorie W. Lundy, Vice President

The Otto S.A. Sprague Memorial Institute
c/o Harris Trust and
Savings Bank
190 South LaSalle Street
Fourth Floor
Chicago, IL 60690
(312) 461-7054

Description: Funding interests include the prevention and relief of human suffering caused by disease.
$ Given: Five grants totaling $600,000; range, $15,000-$190,000
Application: Initial approach by letter
Deadline: None
Contact: Thomas E. Macior

FLOW-THROUGH FUNDING

•　•　•　•　•　•　•　•　•　•　•　•　•　•　•　•　•　•　•

Sundstrand Corporation Foundation
4949 Harrison Avenue
P.O. Box 7003
Rockford, IL 61125
(815) 226-6000

Description: Areas of support include community funds, education, social and health services
$ Given: 112 grants totaling $845,850; range, $450-$122,000
Application: Initial approach by letter
Deadline: None
Contact: Clarence Kieselburg, Secretary

Washington Square Health Foundation
875 North Michigan Avenue
Suite 3516
Chicago, IL 60611
(312) 664-6488

Description: Funds health services, medical research, and medical education
$ Given: 36 grants totaling $812,993; range, $1,000-$200,000
Application: Application form required
Deadline: June 1, December 1
Contact: Howard Nochumson, Executive Director

INDIANA

The Donaldson Foundation
c/o Donaldson Company, Inc.
P.O. Box 1299
Minneapolis, MN 55440
(612) 887-3010

Description: Funding interests include health services, environmental protection, and higher education
$ Given: 98 grants totaling $338,875; range, $300-$38,400
Areas of Support: Illinois, Indiana, Iowa, Kentucky, Minnesota, Missouri, and Wisconsin
Application: Initial approach by letter
Deadline: May 1, August 1
Contact: Raymond Vodovnik, Secretary

Fort Wayne Community Foundation
116 East Wayne Street
Fort Wayne, IN 46802
(219) 426-4083

Description: Areas of support include health services, social services, education, community development, and the arts.
$ Given: 62 grants totaling $295,837; range, $65-$18,000
Application: Initial approach by letter, proposal, or telephone
Deadline: None
Contact: Mrs. Barbara Burt, Executive Director

The Indianapolis Foundation
615 North Alabama Street
Room 119
Indianapolis, IN 46204
(317) 634-7497

Description: Areas of support include health, welfare, and education
$ Given: 84 grants totaling $2,967,065; average range, $4,000-$50,000
Application: Initial approach by letter or telephone
Deadlines: Last day of January, March, May, July, September, or November
Contact: Kenneth I. Chapman, Executive Director

Keebler Company Foundation
One Hollow Tree Lane
Elmhurst, IL 60126
(312) 833-2900

Description: Funding interests include minority programs, health and human services, and education
$ Given: 239 grants totaling $359,987; range, $10-$34,180
Areas of Support: Illinois, Colorado, Indiana, Maine, Minnesota, North Carolina, Pennsylvania, Texas
Application: Initial approach by letter
Deadline: None
Contact: A.G. Bland, Treasurer

E.H. Kilbourne Residuary Charitable Trust
c/o Lincoln National Bank
Trust Department
P.O. Box 9340
Fort Wayne, IN 46899
(219) 461-6451

Description: Funding interests include education, youth agencies, health and social services, and the arts
$ Given: 30 grants totaling $192,558; range, $200-$19,800
Application: Initial approach by letter
Deadline: None
Contact: Alice Kopfer, Vice President

Miles Foundation
1127 Myrtle Street
P.O. Box 40
Elkhart, IN 46515
(219) 264-8225

Description: Areas of support include community funds, education, hospitals and health organizations
Given: 113 grants totaling $511,023; range, $100-$50,000
Application: Initial approach by letter
Deadline: None
Contact: Lehman H. Beardsley, Chairman

FLOW-THROUGH FUNDING

• •

IOWA

John Deere Foundation
John Deere Road
Moline, IL 61265
(309) 765-4137

Description: Areas of support include health services, community funds, youth agencies, and education
$ Given: Grants totaling $3,707,974; range, $300-$539,000
Areas of Support: Iowa, Illinois, Wisconsin
Application: Initial approach by letter
Deadline: None
Contact: Donald R. Morgenthaler, President

The Donaldson Foundation
c/o Donaldson Company, Inc.
P.O. Box 1299
Minneapolis, MN 55440
(612) 887-3010

Description: Funding interests include health services, environmental protection, and higher education
$ Given: 98 grants totaling $338,875; range, $300-$38,400
Areas of Support: Illinois, Indiana, Iowa, Kentucky, Minnesota, Missouri, and Wisconsin
Application: Initial approach by letter
Deadline: May 1, August 1
Contact: Raymond Vodovnik, Secretary

The Hall Foundation, Inc.
115 Third Street SE
No. 803
Cedar Rapids, IA 52401
(319) 362-90779

Description: Funds cultural programs, a community fund, hospitals, and health services
$ Given: 35 grants totaling $3,395,564; range, $500-$680,000
Application: Initial approach by letter
Deadline: None
Contact: John G. Lidvall, Executive Director

Iowa and Illinois Gas and Electric Company Giving Program
206 East Second Street
Davenport, IA 52802
(319) 326-7038

Description: Areas of support include education, health care, child welfare, civic affairs, community development, and family services
$ Given: 186 grants totaling $ 537,065; range, $10-$106,375
Areas of Support: Davenport, Bettendorf, Cedar Rapids, Iowa City, and Fort Dodge, Iowa; Rock Island and Moline, Illinois; and Ohio
Application: Initial approach by letter
Deadline: None
Contact: J.C. Decker, Secretary-Treasurer

• •

**Mid-Iowa Health
Foundation**
550 39th Street
Suite 104
Des Moines, IA 50312
(515) 277-6411

Description: Funds health-related service projects
(including drug abuse, mental health, and nutrution)
$ Given: 41 grants totaling $459,129; range, $700-$27,345
Application: Initial approach by letter
Deadline: February 1, May 1, August 1, and November 1
Contact: Kathryn Bradley

KANSAS

**Arkla Corporate Giving
Program**
400 East Capitol Avenue
P.O. Box 751
Little Rock, AK 72203
(501) 377-4610

Description: Funds a wide variety of programs, including
health services, mental health, AIDS, child welfare and
drug abuse.
$ Given: N/A
Limitations: Giving in major operating areas (Arkansas,
California, Kansas, Texas, Oklahoma, and Mississippi)
Application: Initial approach by letter
Deadline: None
Contact: James L. Rutherford III, Senior Vice President
(Little Rock, Arkansas area) or Hugh H. McCastlain
(Shreveport, Louisiana area)

**Ewing Marion Kauffman
Foundation**
922 Walnut Street
Suite 1100
Kansas City, MO 64106
(816) 966-4000

Description: Funds health agencies, childhood education,
and family services
$ Given: 20 grants totaling $201,639; range, $50-$75,000
Areas of Support: Kansas and Missouri
Application: Brief concept paper
Deadline: None
Contact: Carl Mitchell, Treasurer

**Rice (Ethel and Raymond
F.) Foundation**
700 Massachusetts Street
Lawrence, Kansas 66044
(913) 843-0420

Description: Areas of support include education, health,
youth and social service agencies
$ Given: 80 grants totaling $235,885; range, $500-$16,000
Application: Proposal
Deadline: November 15
Contact: George M. Klem, Treasurer

FLOW-THROUGH FUNDING

• • • • • • • • • • • • • • • • • • • •

KENTUCKY

James Graham Brown Foundation, Inc.
132 East Gray Street
Louisville, KY 40202
(502) 583-4085

Description: Funding interests include community development, health services, and youth
$ Given: 60 grants totaling $8,459,687; range, $100-$1,500,000
Application: Initial approach by letter
Deadline: None
Contact: Mason Rummel, Grants Coordinator

The Cralle Foundation
c/o Liberty National Bank and Trust Co. of Louisville
P.O. Box 32500
Louisville, KY 40232
(502) 566-1702

Description: Funds education, health services, youth groups, community development, and museums
$ Given: 18 grants totaling $785,833; range, $3,500-$300,000
Application: Application form required
Deadline: None
Contact: Institutional Trust Department

The Donaldson Foundation
c/o Donaldson Company, Inc.
P.O. Box 1299
Minneapolis, MN 55440
(612) 887-3010

Description: Funding interests include health services, environmental protection, and higher education
$ Given: 98 grants totaling $338,875; range, $300-$38,400
Areas of Support: Illinois, Indiana, Iowa, Kentucky, Minnesota, Missouri, and Wisconsin
Application: Initial approach by letter
Deadline: May 1, August 1
Contact: Raymond Vodovnik, Secretary

Kentucky Fried Chicken Corporate Giving Program
P.O. Box 32070
Louisville, KY 40232
(502) 456-8300

Description: Funding interests include health services, arts, drug rehabilitation, education, and community development
$ Given: N/A
Application: N/A
Deadline: N/A
Contact: Gregg M. Reynolds, Vice President, Public Affairs

LOUISIANA

The Community Foundation of Shreveport-Bossier
401 Edwards Street
Suite 1520
Shreveport, LA 71101
(318) 221-0582

Description: Funds health services, education, youth agencies, welfare, and cultural programs
$ Given: 41 grants totaling $691,920; range, $170-$100,000
Application: Initial approach by letter
Deadline: March 1, June 1, September 1
Contact: Carol Emanuel, Executive Director

German Protestant Orphan Asylum Association
5342 St. Charles Avenue
New Orleans, LA 70115
(504) 895-2361

Description: Areas of support include medical services, child welfare, family services, and youth programs
$ Given: 18 grants totaling $227,194; range, $1,980-$35,931
Application: Initial approach by letter
Deadline: December, March, June, and September
Contact: Everett T. Aultman, Executive Director

Goldring Family Foundation
809 Jefferson Highway
Jefferson, LA 70121

Description: Funding interests include health services and community funds, with emphasis on Jewish welfare and education
$ Given: 29 grants totaling $384,640; range, $100-$200,000
Application: Application form not required
Deadline: None
Contact: N/A

MAINE

Agnes M. Lindsay Trust
45 Market Street
Manchester, NH 03101
(603) 669-4140

Description: Funding interests include health services, higher education, services for the handicapped, and welfare institutions
$ Given: 191 grants totaling $863,771; average range, $1,000-$10,000
Areas of Support: Maine, Massachusetts, New Hampshire, and Vermont
Application: Proposal
Deadline: None
Contact: Robert L. Chiesa, Trustee

FLOW-THROUGH FUNDING

• •

UNUM Charitable Foundation
2211 Congress Street
Portland, ME 04122
(207) 770-2211

Description: 75% of annual funds go to corporate community grants for health and welfare agencies, arts and cultural programs, education, and civic organizations; 25% to AIDS and aging programs
$ Given: 157 grants totaling $813,833; range, $25-$208,865
Application: Initial approach by letter
Deadline: None
Contact: Judith Nedeau Harrison, Director, Corporate Public Involvement

MARYLAND

The Abell Foundation
1116 Fidelity Building
210 North Charles Street
Baltimore, MD 21201
(301) 547-1300

Description: Funding interests include education, health and family services, arts and culture
$ Given: 188 grants totaling $ 5,650,687; average, $15,000
Application: Initial approach by letter
Deadline: January 1, March 1, May 1, July 1, September 1, November 1
Contact: Robert C. Embry, Jr., President

Bender Foundation, Inc.
1120 Connecticut Avenue NW
Suite 1200
Washington, DC 20036
(202) 828-9000

Description: Funding interests include education, health services, social welfare, Jewish organizations and welfare funds
$ Given: 65 grants totaling $395,200; range, $1,000-$100,000
Areas of Support: Washington, DC, and Maryland
Application: Initial approach by letter
Deadline: November 20
Contact: Sondra D. Bender, President

The Blaustein (Louis and Henrietta) Foundation, Inc.
Blaustein Building
P.O. Box 238
Baltimore, MD 21203

Description: Funding interests include hospitals and health services, music and the arts, education, Jewish welfare funds, and a community fund
$ Given: 29 grants totaling $773,185; range, $500-$360,485
Application: Initial approach by letter
Deadline: None
Contact: Morton K. Blaustein, President

The Columbia Foundation
5430 Vantage Point Road
Columbia, MD 21044
(301) 730-7840

Description: Funding for health and human services, educational programs, housing, and arts and culture
$ Given: 40 grants totaling $382,000; range, $500-$20,000
Application: Initial approach by telephone
Deadline: January, September
Contact: Barbara K. Lawson, Executive Director

The Ryland Group
Corporate Giving Program
10221 Wincopin Circle
P.O. Box 4000
Columbia, MD 21044
(301) 730-7222

Description: Funding interests include cancer, heart disease, and mental health, hunger, programs for the aged, child and family welfare, alcoholism and drug abuse
$ Given: 162 grants totaling $1,100,000; range, $100-$15,000
Application: Initial approach by letter
Deadline: None
Contact: Nancy L. Smith, Vice President, Public Affairs

Signet Bank/Maryland
Giving Program
Marketing-TU307
P.O. Box 1077
Baltimore, MD 21203
(301) 332-5000

Description: Funds arts and culture, civic affairs, education, and health
$ Given: Grants totaling $633,000
Application: N/A
Deadline: N/A
Contact: Corporate Contributions Committee

MASSACHUSETTS

Ansin Foundation
c/o Charles G. Burke
122 Western Avenue
Lowell, MA 01851

Description: Funds health services and hospitals, education, and Jewish giving
$ Given: 15 grants totaling $346,500; range, $1,000-$135,000
Areas of Support: Massachusetts and Pennsylvania
Application: Applications not accepted; giving to pre-selected organizations
Deadline: N/A
Contact: N/A

FLOW-THROUGH FUNDING

· ·

Boston Edison Foundation
800 Boylston Street
P359
Boston, MA 02199
(617) 424-2302

Description: Funds higher education, health and welfare organizations, community development, and arts and cultural programs
$ Given: 97 grants totaling $1,074,230; range, $500-$375,000
Application: Proposal, IRS 501C3 form, annual report, project budget, and contributors list
Deadline: November 1
Contact: Neil F. Doherty, Director

The Boston Globe Foundation II, Inc.
135 Morrissey Boulevard
Boston, MA 02107
(617) 929-3194

Description: Funding interests include education, community services, hospitals and health care, and the media business
$ Given: 499 grants totaling $4,284,715; range, $25-$340,000
Application: Proposal
Deadline: None
Contact: Suzanne Watkin, Executive Director

Donaldson (Oliver S. and Jennie R.) Charitable Trust
c/o Durfee Attleboro Bank, Trust Department
Ten North Main Street
Fall River, MA 02720
(617) 679-8311

Description: Areas of support include cancer research and treatment, hospitals and health agencies, education, and child welfare and youth agencies
$ Given: 37 grants totaling $858,440; range, $1,680-$68,000
Application: Application form required
Deadline: None
Contact: N/A

The Hopedale Foundation
43 Hope Street
Hopedale, MA 01747
(508) 473-0820

Description: Emphasis on area community funds, with support for hospitals, health services, youth agencies, and higher education
$ Given: 22 grants totaling $163,433; range, $1,500-$55,000
Application: Initial approach by letter
Deadline: None
Contact: Thad R. Jackson, Treasurer

• •

**Marion Gardner Jackson
Charitable Trust**
c/o The First National Bank
of Boston
P.O. Box 1861
Boston, MA 02105
(617) 434-5669

Description: Capital funds for youth, health and services,
and arts and cultural programs
$ Given: Grants totaling $239,500
Application: Proposal
Deadline: September 1
Contact: Sharon M. Driscoll, Trust Officer

Agnes M. Lindsay Trust
45 Market Street
Manchester, New Hamp-
shire 03101
(603) 669-4140

Description: Funding interests include health services,
higher education, services for the handicapped, and
welfare institutions
$ Given: 191 grants totaling $863,771; average range,
$1,000-$10,000
Areas of Support: Maine, Massachusetts, New Hampshire, and Vermont
Application: Proposal
Deadline: None
Contact: Robert L. Chiesa, Trustee

Monsanto Fund
800 North Lindbergh
Boulevard
St. Louis, MO 63167
(314) 694-4596

Description: Funding interests include health services,
hospitals, social services, youth, education (science and
mathematics), and community funds
$ Given: Grants totaling $8,285,748; range, $100-$1,112,000
Areas of Support: Alabama, California, Florida, Georgia,
Idaho, Illinois, Massachusetts, Maine, Missouri, New
Jersey, North Carolina, Ohio, South Carolina, Texas, and
West Virginia
Application: Proposal
Deadline: None
Contact: John L. Mason, President

**Shawmut Worcester
County Bank Charitable
Foundation, Inc.**
c/o Shawmut Central Tax
Unit
446 Main Street
Worcester, MA 01608
(617) 793-4401

Description: Funding interests include education, health
and social services, youth agencies, and cultural programs
$ Given: 52 grants totaling $301,350; range, $500-$75,000
Application: Initial approach by letter
Deadline: None
Contact: N/A

FLOW-THROUGH FUNDING

• •

TJX Foundation
c/o TJX Companies
770 Cochituale Road
Framingham, MA 01701
(508) 651-8714

Description: Funds health and social service programs emphasizing women, the elderly, the handicapped, minority groups, and the poor
$ Given: Grants totaling $1,269,975
Application: Proposal
Deadline: None
Contact: Rhonda Boccio

MICHIGAN

ANR Foundation, Inc.
One Woodward Avenue
Detroit, MI 48226
(313) 965-1200

Description: Funds health and welfare, education, culture, and community responsibility
$ Given: 262 grants totaling $1,042,945; range, $13-$89,000
Application: Initial approach by letter
Deadline: None
Contact: James F. Cordes, President

A.G. Bishop Charitable Trust
c/o NDB Genesee Merchants Bank and Trust Company
One East First Street
Flint, MI 48502
(313) 766-8307

Description: Areas of support include health agencies and hospitals, social service and youth agencies, education, and cultural programs
$ Given: 49 grants totaling $227,837; range, $750-$33,300
Application: Initial approach by letter
Deadline: None
Contact: C. Ann Barton, Trust Officer

Herrick Foundation
2500 Comerica Building
Detroit, MI 48226
(313) 963-6420

Description: Funding interests include education (scholarship and capital funds), youth and health service agencies, hospitals, welfare agencies, cultural programs, and Protestant church support
$ Given: 190 grants totaling $10,745,750; range, $500-$1,000,000
Application: Initial approach by letter
Deadline: None
Contact: Catherine R. Cobb

• • • • • • • • • • • • • • • • • • • •

Keebler Company Foundation
One Hollow Tree Lane
Elmhurst, IL 60126
(708) 833-2900

Description: Funding interests include minority programs, health and human services, and education
$ Given: 239 grants totaling $359,987; range, $10-$34,180
Areas of Support: Illinois, Colorado, Indiana, Maine, Minnesota, North Carolina, Pennsylvania, Texas
Application: Initial approach by letter
Deadline: None
Contact: A.G. Bland, Treasurer

Milan (Jack and Florence) Foundation
16500 North Park Drive
Apartment 1708
Southfield, MI 48075

Description: Funds Jewish organizations, health services, and child welfare
$ Given: One grant totaling $105,000
Application: N/A
Deadline: N/A
Contact: N/A

Monsanto Fund
800 North Lindbergh Boulevard
St. Louis, MO 63167
(314) 694-4596

Description: Funding interests include health services, hospitals, social services, youth, education (science and mathematics), and community funds
$ Given: Grants totaling $8,285,748; range, $100-$1,112,000
Areas of Support: Alabama, California, Florida, Georgia, Idaho, Illinois, Massachusetts, Maine, Missouri, New Jersey, North Carolina, Ohio, South Carolina, Texas, and West Virginia
Application: Proposal
Deadline: None
Contact: John L. Mason, President

FLOW-THROUGH FUNDING

. . . .

MINNESOTA

The Blandin Foundation
100 Pokegama Avenue
North
Grand Rapids, MN 55744
(612) 224-5463

Description: Funding interests include leadership development, economic development, health and human services, educational opportunities, the environment, and arts and humanities
$ Given: 467 grants totaling $293,669; range, $167-$2,417
Areas of Support: Rural Minnesota
Application: Initial approach by letter
Deadline: February 1, May 1, August 1, November 1
Contact: Paul M. Olsen, President

Carolyn Foundation
1800 TCF Tower
Minneapolis, MN 55402
(612) 339-7101

Description: Funding for health and welfare, education, culture, women, the environment, and the disadvantaged
$ Given: 37 grants totaling $989,665; range, $1,300-$100,000
Areas of Support: Minneapolis-St. Paul, Minnesota and New Haven, Connecticut
Application: Initial approach by letter
Deadline: January and February for grants under $10,000; January through July for grants over $10,000
Contact: Carol J. Fetzer, Executive Director

Dain Bosworth/IFG Foundation
100 Dain Tower
Minneapolis, MN 55402
(612) 371-2765

Description: Areas of support include health, education, social service, and community funds
$ Given: 510 grants totaling $350,095; range, $25-$56,000
Application: Initial approach by letter
Deadline: January 31, July 31
Contact: Beth James, Executive Director

The Donaldson Foundation
c/o Donaldson Company, Inc.
P.O. Box 1299
Minneapolis, MN 55440
(612) 887-3010

Description: Funding interests include health services, environmental protection, and higher education
$ Given: 98 grants totaling $338,875; range, $300-$38,400
Areas of Support: Illinois, Indiana, Iowa, Kentucky, Minnesota, Missouri, and Wisconsin
Application: Initial approach by letter
Deadline: May 1, August 1
Contact: Raymond Vodovnik, Secretary

Keebler Company Foundation
One Hollow Tree Lane
Elmhurst, IL 60126
(312) 833-2900

Description: Funding interests include minority programs, health and human services, and education
$ Given: 239 grants totaling $359,987; range, $10-$34,180
Areas of Support: Illinois, Colorado, Indiana, Maine, Minnesota, North Carolina, Pennsylvania, Texas
Application: Initial approach by letter
Deadline: None
Contact: A.G. Bland, Treasurer

MISSISSIPPI

Arkla Corporate Giving Program
400 East Capitol Avenue
P.O. Box 751
Little Rock, AK 72203
(501) 377-4610

Description: Funds a wide variety of programs, including health services, mental health, AIDS, child welfare and drug abuse.
$ Given: N/A
Limitations: Giving in major operating areas (Arkansas, California, Kansas, Texas, Oklahoma, and Mississippi)
Application: Initial approach by letter
Deadline: None
Contact: James L. Rutherford III, Senior Vice President (Little Rock, Arkansas area) or Hugh H. McCastlain (Shreveport, Louisiana area)

W.E. Walker Foundation
1675 Lakeland Drive
Riverhill Tower
Suite 400
Jackson, MS 39216
(601) 362-9895

Description: Areas of support include health, cultural programs, youth and welfare agencies, and education
$ Given: 56 grants totaling $2,639,275; average range, $1,000-$15,000
Application: Initial approach by letter
Deadline: None
Contact: W.E. Walker, Jr., Trustee

MISSOURI

The H & R Block Foundation
4410 Main Street
Kansas City, MO 64111
(816) 753-6900

Description: Areas of support include health, the elderly, youth, education, arts and culture, and neighborhood development
$ Given: 246 grants totaling $958,751
Application: Initial approach by letter (1-2 pages)
Deadline: 45 days prior to board meetings (board meets in March, June, September, and December
Contact: Terrence R. Ward, President

FLOW-THROUGH FUNDING

. . . .

The Donaldson Foundation
c/o Donaldson Company, Inc.
P.O. Box 1299
Minneapolis, MN 55440
(612) 887-3010

Description: Funding interests include health services, environmental protection, and higher education
$ Given: 98 grants totaling $338,875; range, $300-$38,400
Areas of Support: Illinois, Indiana, Iowa, Kentucky, Minnesota, Missouri, and Wisconsin
Application: Initial approach by letter
Deadline: May 1, August 1
Contact: Raymond Vodovnik, Secretary

The Green (Allen P. and Josephine B.) Foundation
P.O. Box 523
Mexico, MO 65265
(314) 581-5568

Description: Funds health care and educational programs for children and youth, social services, and arts and other cultural programs
$ Given: 47 grants totaling $500,600; range, $1,000-$30,000
Application: Initial approach by letter
Deadline: April 1, October 1
Contact: Walter G. Staley, Secretary-Treasurer

Group Health Plan Foundation of Greater St. Louis
1056 Caroline Street
St. Louis, MO 63104
(314) 577-8105

Description: Funds health agencies and health services
$ Given: Eight grants totaling $204,975; range, $15,000-$55,000
Application: Initial approach by letter
Deadline: None
Contact: Robert M. Swanson, Secretary

Ewing Marion Kauffman Foundation
922 Walnut Street
Suite 1100
Kansas City, MO 64106
(816) 966-4000

Description: Funds health agencies, childhood education, and family services
$ Given: 20 grants totaling $201,639; range, $50-$75,000
Areas of Support: Kansas and Missouri
Application: Brief concept paper
Deadline: None
Contact: Carl Mitchell, Treasurer

Monsanto Fund
800 North Lindbergh
Boulevard
St. Louis, MO 63167
(314) 694-4596

Description: Funding interests include health services, hospitals, social services, youth, education (science and mathematics), and community funds
$ Given: Grants totaling $8,285,748; range, $100-$1,112,000
Areas of Support: Alabama, California, Florida, Georgia, Idaho, Illinois, Massachusetts, Maine, Missouri, New Jersey, North Carolina, Ohio, South Carolina, Texas, and West Virginia
Application: Proposal
Deadline: None
Contact: John L. Mason, President

Olin (Spencer T. and Ann W.) Foundation
Pierre Laclede Building
7701 Forsyth Boulevard
St. Louis, MO 63105
(314) 727-6202

Description: Funding interests include health services, medical education and research, and community service agencies
$ Given: 23 grants totaling $5,454,050; range, $750-$1,500,000
Application: Initial approach by letter
Deadline: None
Contact: Warren M. Shapleigh, President

Victor E. Speas Foundation
c/o Boatmen's First
National Bank of Kansas
City
14 West Tenth Street
Kansas City, MO 64183

Description: Areas of support include agencies serving the health care needs of youth, elderly, and handicapped
$ Given: 38 grants totaling $1,262,212; range, $1,500-$172,000
Application: Initial approach by telephone
Deadline: None
Contact: David P. Ross, Senior Vice President, Boatmen's First National Bank of Kansas City

Speas (John W. and Effie E.) Foundation
c/o Boatmen's First
National Bank of Kansas
City
14 West Tenth Street
Kansas City, MO 64183

Description: Funds hospitals and health services
$ Given: 28 grants totaling $1,189,129; range, $5,000-$152,000
Application: Initial approach by letter (1-3 pages)
Deadline: None
Contact: David P. Ross, Senior Vice President, Boatmen's First National Bank of Kansas City

FLOW-THROUGH FUNDING

· ·

St. Louis Community Foundation
818 Olive Street
Suite 317
St. Louis, MO 63101
(314) 241-2703

Description: Funding interests include care of the sick, aged, infirm, and handicapped
$ Given: 249 grants totaling $844,231; range, $100 - $200,000
Application: Proposal
Deadline: January 15, April 15, July 15, and October 15
Contact: Mary Brucker, Executive Director

MONTANA

Meyer Memorial Trust
1515 S.W. Fifth Avenue
Suite 500
Portland, OR 97201
(503) 228-5512

Description: General purpose grants in Oregon for education, health and social welfare, arts and humanities; special program grants for Aging and Independence and Support for Children at Risk in Oregon, Alaska, Idaho, Montana, and Washington; operates a Small Grants Program ($500-$8,000) for small projects in Oregon
$ Given: 209 grants totaling $11,953,746; range, $500 - $2,000,000)
Application: Application form required
Deadline: April 1, October 1 for Aging and Independence; July 15, October 15 for Small Grants Program; no deadline for general purpose grants
Contact: Charles S. Rooks, Executive Director

MPCo/Entech Foundation, Inc.
c/o The M-P-Co.
40 East Broadway
Butte, Montana 59701
(406) 723-5421

Description: Funding for human services, youth organizations, hospitals, and health associations
$ Given: 34 grants totaling $310,159; range, $50 - $76,034)
Application: Application form required
Deadline: None
Contact: John Carl, Vice President

NEBRASKA

Thomas D. Buckley Trust
P.O. Box 647
Chappell, NE 69129
(308) 874-2211

Description: Areas of support include health services and hospitals, community development programs, Christian churches, and civic affairs
$ Given: 58 grants totaling $266,736; range, $250 - $35,000)
Application: Initial approach by letter
Deadline: None
Contact: Dwight E. Smith

The IBP Foundation, Inc.
P.O. Box 515
Dakota City, NE 68731
(402) 494-2061

Description: Areas of support include community development and health services
$ Given: Grants totaling $219,916
Application: Application form required
Deadline: None
Contact: George S. Spencer, Chair

The Livingston (Milton S. and Corinne N.) Foundation, Inc.
1125 South 103rd Street
Suite 600
Omaha, NE 68124
(402) 558-1112

Description: Funds local Jewish welfare funds, education, culture, and health services
$ Given: 64 grants totaling $361,522; range, $100 - $100,000)
Application: Initial approach by letter
Deadline: None
Contact: Yale Richards, Executive Director

NEW HAMPSHIRE

Alexandra Eastman Foundation
c/o New Hampshire Charitable Fund
One South Street
P.O. Box 1335
Concord, New Hampshire 03302
(603) 225-6641

Description: Seeks to improve the quality and availability of health care and to promote the health and well-being of residents of the greater Derry, New Hampshire area
$ Given: 13 grants totaling $125,806; range, $2,400 - $30,000)
Application: Initial approach by letter
Deadline: February 1, May 1, August 1, November 1
Contact: Deborah Cowan, Program Director

FLOW-THROUGH FUNDING

. . . .

Foundation for Seacoast Health
P.O. Box 4606
Portsmouth, New Hampshire 03801
(603) 433-4001

Description: Supports and promotes health care for infants, adolescents, and the elderly
$ Given: 32 grants totaling $634,808; range, $500 - $125,000)
Application: Initial approach by letter (2 pages or less)
Deadline: March 1 (infant/child health); June 1 (adolescent health); September 1 (elderly health); December 1 (medical financial assistance)
Contact: N/A

Agnes M. Lindsay Trust
45 Market Street
Manchester, New Hampshire 03101
(603) 669-4140

Description: Funding interests include health services, higher education, services for the handicapped, and welfare institutions
$ Given: 191 grants totaling $863,771 (average range: $1,000-$10,000)
Areas of Support: Maine, Massachusetts, New Hampshire, and Vermont
Application: Proposal
Deadline: None
Contact: Robert L. Chiesa, Trustee

Ellis L. Phillips Foundation
13 Dartmouth College Highway
Lyme, New Hampshire 03768
(603) 795-2790

Description: Areas of support include social services and health care, religion, education, and the arts
$ Given: 38 grants totaling $255,550; range, $600 - $50,000)
Application: Initial approach by letter (1-3 pages)
Deadline: None
Contact: Patricia A. Cate, Executive Director

NEW JERSEY

Campbell Soup Fund
Campbell Place
Camden, New Jersey 08103
(609) 342-6431

Description: Funding interests include hospitals and other health care facilities, cultural programs, education, social service and youth agencies, and community funds
$ Given: 106 grants totaling $1,869,800; range, $1,300 - $200,000)
Areas of Support: Camden, New Jersey and Philadelphia, Pennsylvania
Application: Initial approach by letter
Deadline: None
Contact: Frank G. Moore, Vice-Chair

**CPC International
Corporate Giving Program**
International Plaza
P.O. Box 8000
Englewood Cliffs, New Jersey 07632
(201) 894-2336

Description: Areas of support include education, health and welfare, arts and culture, and community programs
$ Given: Grants totaling $646,148; range, $100 -$22,000)
Application: Initial approach by letter
Deadline: None
Contact: N/A

Hagedorn Fund
c/o Manufacturers Hanover
Trust Company
270 Park Avenue
New York, NY 10017
(212) 270-9107

Description: Funding for education, hospitals and health agencies, the aged, youth agencies, medical research, community funds, and cultural organizations
$ Given: 114 grants totaling $1,110,000; range, $1,000 - $85,000)
Areas of Support: New York metropolitan area (including New Jersey and Connecticut)
Application: Proposal
Deadline: November 15
Contact: Robert Rosenthal, Vice President, Manufacturers Hanover Trust Company

The Hoyt Foundation
Half Acre Road
Cranbury, New Jersey 08512
(201) 872-2322

Description: Areas of support include health service agencies, hospitals, the handicapped, and education, with emphasis on medical education and research
$ Given: 13 grants totaling $147,000; range, $100 - $38,000)
Application: Initial approach by letter
Deadline: None
Contact: Charles O. Hoyt, President

FLOW-THROUGH FUNDING

• •

Jaqua Foundation
One Garrett Mountain Plaza
West Paterson, New Jersey
07424
(201) 278-9790

Description: Funds higher education, hospitals, and health services
$ Given: 23 grants totaling $264,900; range, $2,500 - $35,000)
Application: Initial approach by letter
Deadline: None
Contact: Eli Hoffman, Chair

The Large Foundation
c/o Large, Scammell and
Danziger
117 Main Street
Flemington, New Jersey
08822

Description: Areas of support include health agencies, social service and youth agencies, and historic preservation
$ Given: 39 grants totaling $378,000; range, $500 - $125,000)
Application: Initial approach by letter
Deadline: Prior to annual meeting (October)
Contact: N/A

Monsanto Fund
800 North Lindbergh
Boulevard
St. Louis, MO 63167
(314) 694-4596

Description: Funding interests include health services, hospitals, social services, youth, education (science and mathematics), and community funds
$ Given: Grants totaling $8,285,748; range, $100-$1,112,000
Areas of Support: Alabama, California, Florida, Georgia, Idaho, Illinois, Massachusetts, Maine, Missouri, New Jersey, North Carolina, Ohio, South Carolina, Texas, and West Virginia
Application: Proposal
Deadline: None
Contact: John L. Mason, President

George A. Ohl, Jr., Trust
c/o First Fidelity Bank,
N.A., New Jersey
765 Broad Street
Newark, New Jersey 07102
(201) 430-4237

Description: Funding interests include hospitals and health service agencies, youth projects, and the homeless
$ Given: 38 grants totaling $278,571; range, $500 - $93,651)
Application: Proposal
Deadline: None
Contact: N/A

• • • • • • • • • • • • • • • • • • • •

Petrie Foundation
70 Enterprise Avenue
Secaucus, New Jersey 07094

Description: Areas of support include cultural programs, religious freedom, hospitals and health services, including physical rehabilitation
$ Given: 67 grants totaling $758,170; range, $500 - $108,500)
Application: N/A
Deadline: N/A
Contact: N/A

The Rosenhaus (Sarah and Matthew) Peace Foundation
Picatinny Road
Morristown, New Jersey 07960
(201) 267-6583

Description: Promotes world peace and understanding with emphasis on medical research and health services, Jewish organizations, and higher education
$ Given: 39 grants totaling $678,000; range, $200 - $100,000)
Areas of Support: New Jersey, New York
Application: Applications not accepted; giving to pre-selected organizations
Deadline: N/A
Contact: Irving Rosenhaus, Managing Director

Union Camp Charitable Trust
c/o Union Camp Corporation
1600 Valley Road
Wayne, New Jersey 07470
(201) 628-2248

Description: Areas of support include community funds, higher education, hospitals and health services, and cultural programs
$ Given: Grants totaling $1,728,075 (average range: $2,000-$5,000)
Application: Initial approach by letter
Deadline: January through August
Contact: Sydney N. Phin, Director, Human Resources

The Van Houten (Edward W. and Stella C.) Charitable Trust
c/o First Fidelity Bank, N.A., New Jersey
765 Broad Street
Newark, New Jersey 07102
(201) 430-4536

Description: Funds human services, health care and hospitals (preference given to pediatrics), the disabled, and the elderly
$ Given: Grants totaling $1,000,000 (average range: $10,000-$100,000)
Application: Proposal
Deadline: February 15, May 15, August 15, November 15
Contact: James S. Hohn, Assistant Vice President, First Fidelity Bank

FLOW-THROUGH FUNDING

. . . .

NEW MEXICO

FHP Foundation
401 East Ocean Boulevard
Suite 206
Long Beach, CA 90802
(310) 590-8655

Description: Funds direct delivery of health care services, including education programs, programs for the elderly and chronically ill, and primary care projects in underserved areas.
$ Given: 17 grants totaling $773,064; range, $2,900 - $89,000)
Areas of Support: Giving in southern California, Utah, New Mexico, Arizona
Application: Initial approach by letter
Deadline: February 15, May 15, August 15, and November 15
Contact: Sandra Lund Gavin, Executive Director

NEW YORK

Albany's Hospital for Incurables
P.O. Box 3628
Executive Park
Albany, NY 12203
(518) 459-7711

Description: Seeks to facilitate development of better health care, including the funding of nursing homes, hospitals, hospices, community health centers, regional health planning groups, and medical colleges
$ Given: 17 grants totaling $249,000; range, $3,000-$30,000
Application: Application form required; initial contact by phone or letter
Deadlines: One month before board meetings (board meets in January, April, June, and November)
Contact: Arnold Cogswell, President

The Annenberg Fund, Inc.
St. Davids Center
150 Radnor Chester Road
Suite A 200
St. Davids, PA 19087
(215) 341-9270

Description: Funding interests include education, health and medical research, community service, and cultural programs
$ Given: 150 grants totaling $6,020,616; range, $100-$1,666,667
Application: Applications not accepted; giving to pre-selected organizations
Deadline: N/A
Contact: Alice C. Cory, Secretary-Treasurer

. . . .

Arkell Hall Foundation, Inc.
66 Montgomery Street
Canajoharie, NY 13317
(518) 673-2281

Description: Operates a residence for needy elderly women who are residents of Montgomery County; funds education, health, and social services
$ Given: 78 grants totaling $618,764; range, $500 - $73,633
Application: Form not required
Deadline: September 15
Contact: Joseph A. Santangelo, Administrator

The Barker Welfare Foundation
P.O. Box 2
Glen Head, NY 11545
(516) 759-5592

Description: Funds established organizations in the areas of health services and rehabilitation, child welfare and youth agencies, arts and culture, libraries, family planning, and others
$ Given: 200 grants totaling $1,582,000; range, $1,000 - $50,000
Application: Form not required
Deadline: February 1
Contact: Mrs. Walter L. Ross II, President

The Albert C. Bostwick Foundation
Hillside Avenue and Bacon Road
P.O. Box A
Westbury, NY 11568
(516) 334-5566

Description: Funds hospitals, health service agencies, handicapped, youth agencies, and medical research
$ Given: 46 grants totaling $114,450; range, $150 - $25,000
Application: Initial approach by letter
Deadline: None
Contact: Eleanor P. Bostwich, Trustee

The Brody (Carolyn and Kenneth D.) Foundation
c/o Goldman Sachs and Company
Tax Department
85 Broad Street
New York, NY 10004

Description: Areas of support include health services, education, cultural programs, and hospitals
$ Given: 99 grants totaling $247,838; range, $15 - $25,000
Application: Contributes to pre-selected organizations
Deadline: N/A
Contact: N/A

FLOW-THROUGH FUNDING

. . . .

Central New York Community Foundation, Inc.
600 South Salina Street
Suite 428
Syracuse, NY 13202
(315) 422-9538

Description: Funds existing agencies for health, welfare, educational, recreational, or cultural purposes
$ Given: 324 grants totaling $2,512,360; average range, $200-$15,000
Application: Application form required
Deadlines: 6 weeks before board meetings (board meets March, May, September, and December)
Contact: Margaret G. Ogden, President

Charina Foundation, Inc.
85 Broad Street
New York, NY 10004

Description: Areas of support include arts and culture, health services, community development, welfare funds, recreation, and Jewish organizations
$ Given: 244 grants totaling $504,602; range, $100-$85,000
Application: Applications not accepted; giving to preselected organizations
Deadline: N/A
Contact: Richard L. Menschel, President

The Cohen (Saul Z. and Amy Scheuer) Family Foundation, Inc.
c/o 61 Associates
350 Fifth Avenue
Suite 3410
New York, NY 10118

Description: Funds education, Jewish giving, culture, and health services, including mental health
$ Given: 106 grants totaling $2,580,289; range, $50-$1,000,000
Application: Applications not accepted; giving to preselected organizations
Deadline: N/A
Contact: N/A

The Commonwealth Fund
One East 75th Street
New York, NY 10021
(212) 535-0400

Description: Areas of support include improving health care service, advancing the well-being of elderly people, developing the capabilities of high school students, and improving the health of minorities
$ Given: Grants totaling $9,622,513; range, $1,000-$595,000
Application: Application form not required; initial approach by letter
Deadline: None
Contact: Adrienne E. Fisher, Grants Manager

The Dreyfus (Max and Victoria) Foundation, Inc.
575 Madison Avenue
New York, NY 10022
(212) 605-0354

Description: Areas of support include health and social services, the aged, handicapped, youth, and cultural programs
$ Given: 225 grants totaling $1,547,416; range, $1,000-$30,000
Application: Initial approach by letter
Deadlines: 10 weeks prior to board meetings (mid-February, June, and October)
Contact: Ms. Lucy Gioia, Administrative Assistant

The Favrot Fund
909 Wirt Road
No. 101
Houston, TX 77024
(713) 956-4009

Description: Focus on community-based programs directed toward health, the needy, and the arts
$ Given: 24 grants totaling $310,000; range, $2,000-$25,000
Areas of Support: Texas, California, New York, and Washington, DC
Application: Initial approach by letter
Deadline: None
Contact: Mrs. Carol Parker

FLOW-THROUGH FUNDING

. . . .

**The Glickenhaus
Foundation**
100 Dorchester Road
Scarsdale, NY 10583
(212) 953-7800

Description: Funds social welfare, health services, and international peace organizations
$ Given: 222 grants totaling $433,392; range, $16-$100,000
Application: Proposal
Deadline: None
Contact: N/A

Hagedorn Fund
c/o Manufacturers Hanover
Trust Company
270 Park Avenue
New York, NY 10017
(212) 270-9107

Description: Funding for education, hospitals and health agencies, the aged, youth agencies, medical research, community funds, and cultural organizations
$ Given: 114 grants totaling $1,110,000; range, $1,000-$85,000
Areas of Support: New York metropolitan area (including New Jersey and Connecticut)
Application: Proposal
Deadline: November 15
Contact: Robert Rosenthal, Vice President, Manufacturers Hanover Trust Company

**The John A. Hartford
Foundation, Inc.**
55 East 59th Street
New York, NY 10022
(212) 832-7788

Description: Areas of support include aging and health, and health care cost and quality
$ Given: 75 grants totaling $7,335,587; range, $5,000-$600,000
Application: Initial approach by letter or proposal
Deadline: 6 months prior to funding requirements
Contact: Richard S. Sharpe, Program Director

**The Howard and Bush
Foundation, Inc.**
85 Gillett Street
Hartford, CT 06105
(203) 236-8595

Description: Funding emphasis includes health services
$ Given: 77 grants totaling $1,346,985; range, $3,500-$72,052
Areas of Support: Hartford, Connecticut, and Troy, New York
Application: Initial approach by letter
Deadline: February 1, June 1, October 1
Contact: Nancy Roberts

The Hoyt Foundation
Half Acre Road
Cranbury, NJ 08512
(201) 872-2322

Description: Areas of support include health service
agencies, hospitals, the handicapped, and education, with
emphasis on medical education and research
$ Given: 13 grants totaling $147,000; range, $100-$38,000
Application: Initial approach by letter
Deadline: None
Contact: Charles O. Hoyt, President

**Sid Jacobson Foundation,
Inc.**
151 Sunnyside Boulevard
Plainview, NY 11803

Description: Funds Jewish concerns, health services,
hospitals and medical research
$ Given: 88 grants totaling $225,900; range, $10-$125,000
Application: Application form not required
Deadline: None
Contact: Sid Jacobson, Trustee

**Kennedy (Karen A. and
Kevin W.) Foundation**
Tax Department
85 Broad Street
New York, NY 10004

Description: Areas of support include health services and
community funds
$ Given: 33 grants totaling $141,700; range, $100-$100,000
Application: Applications not accepted; giving to pre-
selected organizations
Deadline: N/A
Contact: N/A

**Key Food Stores
Foundation, Inc.**
8925 Avenue D
Brooklyn, NY 11236
(212) 510-5502

Description: Areas of support include Jewish giving,
health, hospitals, and health clinics
$ Given: 29 grants totaling $110,585; range, $25-$69,000
Application: Application form not required
Deadline: None
Contact: Allen Newman, Trustee

FLOW-THROUGH FUNDING

* * * * * * * * * * * * * * * * * * * *

The Klau (David and Sadie) Foundation
c/o Rochlin, Lipsky, Goodkin, Stoler and Co., P.C.
510 Fifth Avenue
New York, NY 10036
(212) 840-6444

Description: Funding interests include health, AIDS, education, Jewish welfare funds, child development, and human services
$ Given: 164 grants totaling $649,249; range, $10-$200,000
Application: Initial approach by letter
Deadline: None
Contact: Sadie K. Klau, President

Klock Company Trust
c/o Key Trust Company
253 Wall Street
Kingston, NY 12401
(914) 339-6750

Description: Areas of support include health services, hospitals, social services, youth agencies, education, and cultural programs
$ Given: 28 grants totaling $221,965; range, $1,000-$25,000
Areas of Support: Kingston and Ulster Counties, New York
Application: Initial approach by letter
Deadlines: March, June, September, and December 31
Contact: Earle H. Foster

The Langeloth (Jacob and Valeria) Foundation
One East 42nd Street
New York, NY 10017
(212) 687-3760

Description: Funds non-profit hospitals and health care facilities to defray costs incurred by in-patients who are "people of education" or in the arts who normally would not be justified in accepting charity but who nonetheless would have difficulty meeting their obligations
$ Given: 25 grants totaling $1,451,000; range, $15,000-$100,000
Application: Applications from previous recipients only
Deadline: September 1
Contact: William R. Cross, Jr., President

The Lincoln Fund
292 Madison Avenue
24th Floor
New York, NY 10017
(212) 889-4109

Description: Areas of support include aid to the elderly, education, nursing and medical programs
$ Given: 19 grants totaling $285,000; range, $5,000-$25,000
Application: Initial approach by letter
Deadline: None
Contact: Mrs. James Sargent, President

**J.M. McDonald
Foundation, Inc.**
2057 East River Road
Cortland, NY 13045
(607) 756-9283

Description: Funding interests include the aged, orphans, child welfare, education, health and hospitals
$ Given: 26 grants totaling $405,000; range, $2,500-$30,000
Application: Applications not accepted; giving to pre-selected organizations
Deadline: N/A
Contact: N/A

Frederick McDonald Trust
c/o Norstar Trust Company
69 State Street
Albany, NY 12201
(518) 447-4189

Description: Funds hospitals and health service agencies, youth agencies, and a community fund
$ Given: 33 grants totaling $129,500; range, $1,000-$20,000
Application: Application form required
Deadline: October 1
Contact: R.F. Galvin, Senior Trust Officer

Metzger-Price Fund, Inc.
230 Park Avenue
New York, NY 10169
(212) 867-9500

Description: Areas of support include health services, the handicapped, the elderly, child welfare and social service agencies
$ Given: 114 grants totaling $201,000; range, $500-$5,000
Application: Initial approach by letter
Deadlines: One month prior to board meetings (board meets in January, April, July, and October)
Contact: Marie Mallot, Secretary-Treasurer

FLOW-THROUGH FUNDING

. . . .

Morgan Guaranty Trust Company of New York Charitable Trust
60 Wall Street
New York, NY 10260
(212) 648-9673

Description: Areas of support include chronic care management, school health services, and women's centers
$ Given: 349 grants totaling $6,597,039; range, $500-$400,000
Application: Proposal
Deadline: September 15
Contact: Roberta Ruocco, Vice President

New York Foundation
350 Fifth Avenue
No. 2901
New York, NY 10118
(212) 549-8009

Description: Areas of support include programs for the elderly and health services
$ Given: 88 grants totaling $2,318,000; range, $10,000-$50,000
Application: Initial approach by letter
Deadlines: November 1, March 1, and July 1
Contact: Madeline Lee, Executive Director

William S. Paley Foundation, Inc.
51 West 52nd Street
Room 3490
New York, NY 10019
(212) 765-3333

Description: Areas of support include Museum of Television and Radio, education, health services and hospitals, and cultural programs
$ Given: 49 grants totaling $755,150; range, $150-$275,000
Application: Proposal
Deadline: None
Contact: Patrick S. Gallagher, Assistant Secretary

Rochester Area Foundation
335 Main Street East
Suite 402
Rochester, NY 14604
(716) 325-4353

Description: Areas of support include education, health services, cultural programs, and community development
$ Given: 593 grants totaling $1,831,842; range, $100-$80,000
Application: Initial approach by letter
Deadline: Board meets in January, March, May, July, September, and November
Contact: Linda S. Weinstein, President

**Helena Rubenstein
Foundation, Inc.**
405 Lexington Avenue
New York, NY 10174
(212) 896-0806

Description: Emphasis on projects that benefit women and children, including health, community, and social services, and education and the arts
$ Given: Grants totaling $5,035,518; range, $1,500-$300,000
Application: Initial approach by letter
Deadline: None
Contact: Diane Moss, Executive Director

**The Spingold (Nate B.
and Frances) Foundation,
Inc.**
c/o Lankenau and Bickford
1740 Broadway
New York, NY 10019

Description: Areas of support include health and human services, with focus on pediatric, geriatric, and gerontological needs
$ Given: Six grants totaling $222,400; range, $12,400-$75,000
Application: Proposal
Deadline: None
Contact: Daniel L. Kurtz, President

**The Seth Sprague
Educational and
Charitable Foundation**
c/o U.S. Trust Company of
New York
114 West 147th Street
New York, NY 10036
(212) 852-3683

Description: Areas of support include health and human services, culture and the arts, education, and community development
$ Given: 386 grants totaling $1,560,000; range, $1,000-$25,000
Application: Initial approach by letter
Deadline: April 15, October 15
Contact: Maureen Augusciak, Senior Vice President

FLOW-THROUGH FUNDING

. . . .

**Amy Plant Satter
Foundation**
598 Madison Avenue
9th Floor
New York, NY 10022

Description: Funding interests include health agencies
and hospitals, and social services
$ Given: 43 grants totaling $138,000; range, $1,000-$5,000
Application: Initial approach by letter
Deadline: None
Contact: John H. Reilly, Jr., Trustee

**Stern (Bernie and Milton)
Foundation**
335 Madison Avenue
New York, NY 10017
(212) 503-1701

Description: Areas of support include health services,
Jewish welfare, and social services
$ Given: 28 grants totaling $239,167; range, $100-$20,000
Application: Application form required
Deadline: N/A
Contact: Bernice Stern, Vice President

Utica Foundation, Inc.
270 Genesee Street
Utica, NY 13502
(315) 735-8212

Description: Funds social and health services, scholar-
ship programs, and cultural programs
$ Given: 44 grants totaling $316,577; range, $700-$72,500
Application: Initial approach by letter
Deadline: N/A
Contact: N/A

**Voute (Mary Jane and
William J.) Foundation,
Inc.**
c/o Salomon Brothers, Inc.
One New York Plaza
New York, NY 10004

Description: Funding interests include Catholic church,
education, health and social services
$ Given: 82 grants totaling $377,255; range, $10-$30,000
Application: Applications not accepted; giving to pre-
selected organizations
Deadline: N/A
Contact: N/A

. . . .

Lawrence A. Wein Foundation, Inc.
c/o Wein, Malkin and Bettex
60 East 42nd Street
New York, NY 10165

Description: Areas of support include education, Jewish religious and social organizations and welfare funds, health services and hospitals, cultural programs, and social services
$ Given: 275 grants totaling $1,516,020
Application: Initial approach by letter
Deadline: N/A
Contact: Lawrence A. Wein, President

NORTH CAROLINA

Champion McDowell Davis Charitable Foundation
2405 Oleander Drive
Wilmington, NC 28403

Description: Funds health services, care for the elderly, and conservation
$ Given: Six grants totaling $146,870; range, $1,000-$130,000
Application: Initial approach by letter
Deadline: N/A
Contact: Michael C. Brown, President

Close Foundation, Inc.
P.O. Drawer 460
104 East Springs Street
Lancster, SC 29720
(803) 286-2196

Description: Areas of support include health care and community services, education, and recreation
$ Given: 25 grants totaling $391,340; range, $500-$60,000
Areas of Support: Lancaster County, Chester Township of Chester County, Fort Mill Township, South Carolina, and North Carolina
Application: Proposal
Deadline: None
Contact: Charles A. Bundy, President

Community Foundation of Gaston County, Inc.
P.O. Box 123
Gastonia, NC 28053
(704) 864-0927

Description: Funds arts, educations, health services, museums, and medical grants to children under 19
$ Given: Grants totaling $484,656
Application: Initial approach by letter
Deadlines: February 15, August 15
Contact: Rebecca B. Carter, Executive Director

FLOW-THROUGH FUNDING

• •

The Dover Foundation
P.O. Box 208
Shelby, NC 28150
(704) 847-2000

Description: Funding interests include health services, education, church support, museums, and social service agencies
$ Given: 1135 grants totaling $545,000; range, $100-$250,000
Application: Initial approach by letter
Deadline: July
Contact: Hoyt Q. Bailey, President

The Fullerton Foundation, Inc.
P.O. Box 1146
Gaffney, SC 29342
(803) 489-6678

Description: Funds hospitals, health care, and medical research
$ Given: 34 grants totaling $1,203,000; range, $1,000-$132,900
Areas of Support: South Carolina and North Carolina
Application: Initial approach by letter
Deadline: April 1, August 1
Contact: Walter E. Cavell, Executive Director

James G. Hanes Memorial Fund/Foundation
c/o Wachovia Bank and
Trust Company, N.A.
P.O. Box 3099
MC31022
Winston-Salem, NC 27150
(919) 770-5274

Description: Funds health and education projects, conservation, community programs, and cultural programs
$ Given: 39 grants totaling $1,033,830; range, $1,000-$380,000
Application: Proposal
Deadlines: March 15, June 15, September 15, and December 15
Contact: Joyce T. Adger, Vice President, Wachovia Bank and Trust Company

Harris (James J. and Angelia M.) Foundation
P.O. Box 220427
Charlotte, NC 28222
(704) 364-6046

Description: Funding interests include education, health services, Presbyterian churches, and youth and social service agencies
$ Given: 52 grants totaling $755,062; range, $1,000-$50,000
Application: Initial approach by letter (max. three pages)
Deadline: None
Contact: Lillian Seaman

• • • • • • • • • • • • • • • • • • • •

**Keebler Company
Foundation**
One Hollow Tree Lane
Elmhurst, IL 60126
(312) 833-2900

Description: Funding interests include minority programs, health and human services, and education
$ Given: 239 grants totaling $359,987; range, $10-$34,180
Areas of Support: Illinois, Colorado, Indiana, Michigan, Minnesota, North Carolina, Pennsylvania, Texas
Application: Initial approach by letter
Deadline: None
Contact: A.G. Bland, Treasurer

Monsanto Fund
800 North Lindbergh
Boulevard
St. Louis, Missouri 63167
(314) 694-4596

Description: Funding interests include health services, hospitals, social services, youth, education (science and mathematics), and community funds
$ Given: Grants totaling $8,285,748; range, $100-$1,112,000
Areas of Support: Alabama, California, Florida, Georgia, Idaho, Illinois, Massachusetts, Michigan, Missouri, New Jersey, North Carolina, Ohio, South Carolina, Texas, and West Virginia
Application: Proposal
Deadline: None
Contact: John L. Mason, President

**Kate B. Reynolds
Charitable Trust**
BB & T Building
Eight West Third Street
Suite M3
Winston-Salem, NC 27101
(919) 723-1456

Description: 75% of income goes to health care for those in need statewide, including services for the aged and those with cancer
$ Given: 97 grants totaling $12,628,574; range, $5,000-$4,500,000
Application: Proposal
Deadline: April 1, October 1
Contact: W. Vance Frye, Executive Secretary

NORTH DAKOTA

**Leach (Tom and Frances)
Foundation**
P.O. Box 1136
Bismarck, ND 58502
(701) 255-0479

Description: Areas of support include education, hospitals and health services, social service and youth agencies, and cultural programs
$ Given: 41 grants totaling $254,500; range, $500-$50,000
Application: Initial approach by letter
Deadline: October 1
Contact: Clement C. Webster, Executive Director

FLOW-THROUGH FUNDING

. . . .

OHIO

Coshocton Foundation
P.O. Box 15
Coshocton, OH 43812
(614) 622-2532

Description: Funding interests include community improvement, health services, education, and a museum
$ Given: Grants totaling $283,311; range, $1,000-$15,125
Application: Initial approach by letter
Deadline: None
Contact: Orville Fuller, Treasurer

Dana Corporation Foundation
P.O. Box 1000
Toledo, OH 43697
(419) 535-4500

Description: Areas of support include community funds, education, health and social services, youth agencies, and cultural programs
$ Given: 232 grants totaling $1,529,526; range, $100-$161,340
Application: Proposal
Deadline: None
Contact: Pauline Marzollini, Assistant Secretary

The Dayton Foundation
2100 Kettering Tower
Dayton, OH 45423
(513) 222-0410

Description: Areas of support include cultural programs, health and social services, community development, and youth
$ Given: 361 grants totaling $2,232,013; range, $25-$506,501
Application: Initial approach by letter or telephone
Deadlines: March, July, September, and November
Contact: Marilyn Kaplan, Administrative Officer

The Eaton Charitable Fund
Eaton Center
Cleveland, OH 44114
(216) 523-4822

Description: Funding interests include health and human services, medical research, civic and cultural organizations, and independent college funds
$ Given: Grants totaling $3,670,904; average range, $1,000-$10,000
Areas of support include: Areas of company operations
Application: Initial approach by letter or proposal
Deadline: None
Contact: Frederick B. Unger, Director of Community Affairs

• • • • • • • • • • • • • • • • • • • •

The S.N. Ford and Ada Ford Fund
c/o Trustcorp Bank, Ohio
42 North Main
Mansfield, OH 44902
(419) 526-3493

Description: Assistance to the aged and the sick; scholarships to the youth of Richland County, Ohio
$ Given: 10 organization grants totaling $36,100; range, $1,000-$7,500; 392 grants to individuals totaling $298,348; range, $16-$11,472
Application: Initial approach by telephone
Deadline: None
Contact: N/A

Iowa and Illinois Gas and Electric Company Giving Program
206 East Second Street
Davenport, IA 52802
(319) 326-7038

Description: Areas of support include education, health care, child welfare, civic affairs, community development, and family services
$ Given: 186 grants totaling $ 537,065; range, $10-$106,375
Areas of Support: Davenport, Bettendorf, Cedar Rapids, Iowa City, and Fort Dodge, Iowa; Rock Island and Moline, Illinois; and Ohio
Application: Initial approach by letter
Deadlines: Board meets in January, April, July, and October
Contact: J.C. Decker, Secretary-Treasurer

The Kangesser (Robert E., Harry A., and M. Sylvia) Foundation
1801 East 9th Street
No. 1220
Cleveland, OH 44114
(216) 621-5747

Description: Areas of support include Jewish educational organizations, non-denominational health and medical services, and civic affairs
$ Given: 23 grants totaling $320,000; range, $200-$150,000
Application: Proposal
Deadline: August 31
Contact: David G. Kangesser, President

William H. Kilcawley Fund
c/o The Dollar Savings and Trust Company
P.O. Box 450
Youngstown, OH 44501

Description: Funding interests include programs for the aged and homeless, health and social services, Christian churches, education, and community funds
$ Given: 19 grants totaling $373,700; range, $500-$110,000
Application: Initial approach by letter
Deadline: None
Contact: N/A

FLOW-THROUGH FUNDING

•   •

The Lincoln Electric Foundation
c/o Society National Bank
22801 St. Clair Avenue
Cleveland, OH 44117
(216) 481-8100

Description: Areas of support include education, a community fund, hospitals and medical services, social service agencies, civic institutions, and cultural programs
$ Given: 40 grants totaling $477,750; range, $250-$115,000
Application: Initial approach by letter
Deadline: September 20
Contact: Ellis F. Smolik, Secretary-Treasurer

David Meade Massie Trust
65 East Second Street
P.O. Box 41
Chillicothe, OH 45601
(614) 772-5070

Description: Funds community development, youth, health, and social service agencies, education, and cultural programs
$ Given: 55 grants totaling $235,671; range, $750-$5,000
Application: Application form required
Deadlines: March 15, June 15, September 15, and December 15
Contact: Marilyn Carnes

Monsanto Fund
800 North Lindbergh Boulevard
St. Louis, Missouri 63167
(314) 694-4596

Description: Funding interests include health services, hospitals, social services, youth, education (science and mathematics), and community funds
$ Given: Grants totaling $8,285,748; range, $100-$1,112,000
Areas of Support: Alabama, California, Florida, Georgia, Idaho, Illinois, Massachusetts, Michigan, Missouri, New Jersey, North Carolina, Ohio, South Carolina, Texas, and West Virginia
Application: Proposal
Deadline: None
Contact: John L. Mason, President

Ohio Bell Foundation
45 Erieview Plaza
Room 870
Cleveland, OH 44114
(216) 822-2423

Description: Funds civic affairs, community development, health, higher, secondary and elementary education, and art and culture
$ Given: 400 grants totaling $2,382,947; range, $100-$500,000
Application: Proposal
Deadline: None
Contact: William W. Boag, Executive Director

The Elisabeth Severance Prentiss Foundation
c/o National City Bank
P.O. Box 5756
Cleveland, OH 44101
(216) 575-2760

Description: Areas of support include hospitals and health institutions in Cuyahoga County, Ohio that are organized and operated exclusively for public charitable purposes
$ Given: 19 grants totaling $2,647,641; range, $5,000-$1,228,740
Application: Proposal
Deadlines: Before May 15 and November 15
Contact: Frank Dinda

P.K. Ranney Foundation
1525 National City Bank
Building
Cleveland, OH 44144
(216) 696-4200

Description: Funds a local community foundation, health services, and marine sciences
$ Given: 10 grants totaling $250,000; range, $5,000-$150,000
Application: Proposal
Deadline: None
Contact: Phillip K. Ranney, Secretary

The Richland County Foundation of Mansfield, Ohio
34 1/2 South Park Street
Room 202
Mansfield, OH 44902
(419) 525-3020

Description: Areas of support include health services, hospital additions, education, programs for the indigent aged, youth programs, the handicapped, and the local community fund
$ Given: 43 grants totaling $865,278; range, $35-$187,240
Application: Proposal
Deadline: None
Contact: Betty J. Crawford, Executive Director

FLOW-THROUGH FUNDING

. . . .

The Stouffer Corporation Fund
29800 Bainbridge Road
Solon, OH 44139
(216) 248-3600

Description: Funds higher education, health, community funds, and cultural programs
$ Given: 277 grants totaling $402,550; range, $100-$77,500
Application: Initial approach by letter
Deadline: None
Contact: N/A

Watson (Walter E. and Caroline H.) Foundation
P.O. Box 450
Youngstown, OH 44501
(216) 744-9000

Description: Funding interests include education, community development, health and human services, child development and youth agencies, and arts and cultural programs
$ Given: 47 grants totaling $238,319; range, $500-$46,000
Application: Application form not required
Deadline: None
Contact: Herbert H. Pridham

OKLAHOMA

Arkla Corporate Giving Program
400 East Capitol Avenue
P.O. Box 751
Little Rock, AK 72203
(501) 377-4610

Description: Funds a wide variety of programs, including health services, mental health, AIDS, child welfare and drug abuse.
$ Given: N/A
Areas of Support: Giving in major operating areas (Arkansas, California, Kansas, Texas, Oklahoma, and Mississippi)
Application: Initial approach by letter
Deadline: None
Contact: James L. Rutherford III, Senior Vice President (Little Rock, Arkansas area) or Hugh H. McCastlain (Shreveport, Louisiana area)

Fort Howard Foundation, Inc.
P.O. Box 11325
Green Bay, WI 54307
(414) 435-8821

Description: Areas of support include education, health care facilities, cultural programs, and social service and youth agencies
$ Given: 6 grants totaling $726,652; range, $13,700-$150,000
Areas of Support: Green Bay, Wisconsin; Muskogee, Oklahoma; and Effingham County, Georgia
Application: The foundation is not presently making any new funding commitments
Contact: Bruce W. Nagel, Executive Director

Gussman (Herbert and Roseline) Foundation
3200 First National Tower
Tulsa, OK 74103

Description: Areas of support include Jewish giving, health services, cultural programs, and educational institutions
$ Given: 56 grants totaling $312,789; range, $25-$220,201
Application: Applications not accepted; giving to pre-selected organizations
Deadline: N/A
Contact: N/A

The Helmerich Foundation
1579 East 21st Street
Tulsa, OK 74114
(918) 742-5531

Description: Large capital funding to Protestant religious organizations, youth and health service agencies, a community development project, and arts and culture
$ Given: Five grants totaling $1,000,000; range, $50,000-$250,000
Application: Initial approach by letter
Deadline: None
Contact: W.H. Helmerich III, Trustee

Public Service Company of Oklahoma Corporate Giving Program
212 East 6th Street
P.O. Box 201
Tulsa, OK 74119
(918) 599-2000

Description: Funding interests include the elderly, child welfare, culture, alcoholism, and education
$ Given: 250 grants totaling $440,000; range, $100-$130,000
Application: Initial approach by letter
Deadline: None
Contact: William R. Stratton, Vice President and C.F.O.

C.W. Titus Foundation
1801 Philtower Building
Tulsa, OK 74103
(918) 582-8095

Description: Funds hospitals and health services, the handicapped, cultural programs, and social service agencies
$ Given: 43 grants totaling $250,269; range, $1,000-$50,000
Application: Application form not required
Deadline: None
Contact: N/A

FLOW-THROUGH FUNDING

. . . .

The William K. Warren Foundation
P.O. Box 470372
Tulsa, OK 74147
(918) 492-8100

Description: Funds local Catholic health care facilities, education, and social services
$ Given: 32 grants totaling $15,389,470; range, $200-$5,700,000
Application: Initial approach by letter
Deadline: None
Contact: W.R. Lissau, President

The Williams Companies Foundation
P.O. Box 2400
Tulsa, OK 74102
(918) 588-2106

Description: Areas of support include health and human services, education, arts and cultural programs, and civic projects
$ Given: Grants totaling $911,368; range, $50-$387,000
Application: Proposal
Deadline: None
Contact: Hannah D. Robson, Manager

OREGON

The Clark Foundation
255 S.W. Harrison Street
GA 2
Portland, OR 97201
(503) 223-5290

Description: Funding interests include medical care, secondary education, youth agencies, cultural programs, and the environment
$ Given: Grants totaling $492,982
Application: Initial approach by letter
Deadline: None
Contact: Jean Ameele

Collins Medical Trust
1618 S.W. First Avenue
Suite 300
Portland, OR 97201
(503) 227-1219

Description: Funds health services and medical research
$ Given: 12 grants totaling $147,385; range, $1,000-$25,000
Application: Initial approach by letter
Deadline: None
Contact: Joseph A. Connolly, Administrator

. . . .

The William G. Gilmore Foundation
120 Montgomery Street
Suite 1880
San Francisco, CA 94104
(415) 546-1400

Description: Funds community-based organization, including family and social services, health services, and AIDS programs
$ Given: 132 grants totaling $766,345; range, $200-$50,000
Areas of Support: Giving in northern California, Oregon, and Washington.
Application: Initial approach by mail
Deadlines: May 1, November 1
Contact: Faye Wilson, Secretary

Louisiana-Pacific Foundation
111 S.W. Fifth Avenue
Portland, OR 97204
(503) 221-0800

Description: Areas of support include health, youth agencies, community funds, education, and the arts
$ Given: 228 grants totaling $780,169; range, $100-$100,000
Application: Initial approach by letter
Deadline: None
Contact: Robert E. Erickson, Trustee

Meyer Memorial Trust
1515 S.W. Fifth Avenue
Suite 500
Portland, OR 97201
(503) 228-5512

Description: General purpose grants in Oregon for education, health and social welfare, arts and humanities; special program grants for Aging and Independence and Support for Children at Risk in Oregon, Alaska, Idaho, Montana, and Washington; operates a Small Grants Program (500-$8,000) for small projects in Oregon
$ Given: 209 grants totaling $11,953,746; range, $500-$2,000,000
Application: Application form required
Deadline: April 1, October 1 for Aging and Independence; July 15, October 15 for Small Grants Program; no deadline for general purpose grants
Contact: Charles S. Rooks, Executive Director

Wheeler Foundation
1211 S.W. Fifth Avenue
Suite 2906
Portland, OR 97204
(503) 228-0261

Description: Areas of support include higher and secondary education, health and medical services and research, cultural programs, and youth agencies
$ Given: 63 grants totaling $240,125; range, $250-$20,000
Application: Initial approach by letter
Deadline: None
Contact: Samuel C. Wheeler, President

. . . .

PENNSYLVANIA

Bell Telephone Company of Pennsylvania Giving Program
One Parkway
9th Floor "A"
Philadelphia, PA 19102
(215) 466-2257

Description: Funds education, health, welfare, culture and the arts
$ Given: Grants totaling $2,352,947; average range, $1,000-$400,000
Application: Letter, proposal, and IRS 501C3 form demonstrating non-profit status
Deadline: September 30
Contact: Charles D. Fulton, Corporate Contributions Manager

Claude Worthington Benedum Foundation
1400 Benedum-Trees Building
Pittsburgh, PA 15222
(412) 288-0360

Description: Funds education, health and human services, community and economic development, and the arts
$ Given: and 107 grants totaling $7,056,551; range, $3,000-$1,000,000
Areas of Support: West Virginia and Greater Pittsburgh, Pennsylvania
Application: Initial approach by letter or telephone
Deadline: None
Contact: Paul R. Jenkins, President

Campbell Soup Fund
Campbell Place
Camden, NJ 08103
(609) 342-6431

Description: Funding interests include hospitals and other health care facilities, cultural programs, education, social service and youth agencies, and community funds
$ Given: 106 grants totaling $1,869,800; range, $1,300-$200,000
Areas of Support: Camden, New Jersey and Philadelphia, Pennsylvania
Application: Initial approach by letter
Deadline: None
Contact: Frank G. Moore, Vice-Chairman

The Clapp (Anne L. and George H.) Charitable and Educational Trust
c/o Mellon Bank, N.A.
One Mellon Bank Center
Pittsburgh, PA 15230
(412) 234-5598

Description: Areas of support include education, health and social services, hospitals, and a community fund
$ Given: 37 grants totaling $453,500; range, $3,000-$30,000
Application: Initial approach by letter
Deadline: None
Contact: William B. Outy, Vice President, Mellon Bank

Cyclops Foundation
650 Washington Road
Pittsburgh, PA 15228
(412) 343-4000

Description: Areas of support include health services and hospitals, youth and child welfare, the environment, and higher education
$ Given: 56 grants totaling $262,636; range, $500-$50,000
Application: Initial approach by letter
Deadline: None
Contact: Susan R. Knapp, Manager-Cash and Banking

Eden Hall Foundation
Pittsburgh Office and Research Park
5500 Corporate Drive
Suite 210
Pittsburgh, PA 15237

Description: Funding interests include education, the prevention and alleviation of sickness and disease, and the advancement of good morals
$ Given: 71 grants totaling $3,552,000; range, $2,000-$300,000
Application: Initial approach by letter
Deadline: None
Contact: Arthur H. Andersen, Secretary

FLOW-THROUGH FUNDING

. . . .

Fannie Mae Foundation
3900 Wisconsin Avenue,
N.W.
Washington, DC 20016
(202) 752-6500

Description: Funding interests include housing and community development, and health and social concerns
$ Given: 300 grants totaling $1,151,567; range, $100-$50,000
Areas of Support: Washington, DC; Pasadena, California; Atlanta, Georgia; Chicago, Illinois; and Philadelphia, PA
Application: Proposal
Deadline: None
Contact: Harriet M. Ivey, Executive Director

Keebler Company Foundation
One Hollow Tree Lane
Elmhurst, IL 60126
(312) 833-2900

Description: Funding interests include minority programs, health and human services, and education
$ Given: 239 grants totaling $359,987; range, $10-$34,180
Areas of Support: Illinois, Colorado, Indiana, Michigan, Minnesota, North Carolina, Pennsylvania, Texas
Application: Initial approach by letter
Deadline: None
Contact: A.G. Bland, Treasurer

The Lancaster County Fund
Horst Group Building
29 East King Street
Room 14
Lancaster, PA 17602
(717) 397-1629

Description: Funding interests include health services, youth agencies, education, and cultural programs
$ Given: 52 grants totaling $378,012; average range, $3,000-$10,000
Application: Application form required
Deadline: October 15
Contact: Nancy L. Neff, Executive Secretary

John R. McCune Charitable Trust
P.O. Box 1749
Pittsburgh, PA 15230
(412) 644-7664

Description: Funds education, health services, Presbyterian institutions, and social services
$ Given: 63 grants totaling $1,993,900; range, $5,000-$142,500
Application: Proposal
Deadline: May 1
Contact: James M. Edwards, Member, Dispensing Committee

McCune Foundation
1104 Commonwealth
Building
316 Fourth Avenue
Pittsburgh, PA 15222
(412) 644-8779

Description: Areas of support include education, health, social services, and community health centers
$ Given: 37 grants totaling $13,364,994; range, $40,000-$1,500,000
Application: Initial approach by letter
Deadlines: November 1, March 15
Contact: Earland I. Carlson, Executive Director

R.K. Mellon Family Foundation
P.O. Box 1138
Pittsburgh, PA 15230
(412) 392-2800

Description: Funds education, health care, social and human services, and conservation
$ Given: 70 grants totaling $1,103,950; range, $1,000-$100,000
Application: Proposal
Deadlines: April 1, October 1
Contact: Robert B. Burr, Jr., Director

Mine Safety Appliances Company Charitable Trust
c/o Mine Safety Appliances
Company
P.O. Box 426
Pittsburgh, PA 15230

Description: Areas of support include health care, community funds, and education
$ Given: 132 grants totaling $607,818; range, $100-$125,000
Application: Initial approach by letter
Deadline: None
Contact: James E. Herald, Secretary

Pittsburgh National Bank Foundation
Pittsburgh National Building
14th Floor
Fifth Avenue and Wood St.
Pittsburgh, PA 15222
(412) 762-4222

Description: Funds health services and hospitals, community funds, social services, education, and youth agencies
$ Given: 277 grants totaling $1,541,055; range, $25-$363,500
Application: Initial approach by letter
Deadline: None
Contact: D. Paul Beard, Secretary

FLOW-THROUGH FUNDING

• • • • • • • • • • • • • • • • • • • •

Stockpole-Hall Foundation
44 South St. Marys Street
St. Marys, PA 15857
(814) 834-1845

Description: Areas of support include education, youth and child welfare, health services, and community development
$ Given: 54 grants totaling $659,768; range, $800-$53,000
Application: Initial approach by letter
Deadline: None
Contact: William C. Conrad, Executive Secretary

Wilson (Hugh and Mary) Foundation, Inc.
c/o Wood and Seitl
240 North Washington Boulevard
Suite 460
Sarasota, FL 34236
(813) 954-2155

Description: Areas of support include cancer research and health services, the performing arts, and social service issues
$ Given: 26 grants totaling $238,291; range, $1,000-$50,000
Areas of Support: Manatee-Sarasota, Florida; Lewisburg-Danville, Pennsylvania
Application: Initial approach by letter
Deadline: None
Contact: John R. Wood, President

RHODE ISLAND

The Rhode Island Foundation/The Rhode Island Community Foundation
957 North Main Street
Providence, RI 02904
(401) 274-4564

Description: Funding interests include education, health care, the aged, youth, and social services
$ Given: Grants totaling $3,381,921
Application: Initial approach by letter or telephone
Deadline: None
Contact: Douglas M. Jansson, Executive Director

SOUTH CAROLINA

Close Foundation, Inc.
P.O. Drawer 460
104 East Springs Street
Lancster, SC 29720
(803) 286-2196

Description: Areas of support include health care (including cancer) and community services, education, and recreation
$ Given: 25 grants totaling $391,340; range, $500-$60,000
Areas of Support: Lancaster County, Chester Township of Chester County, Fort Mill Township, South Carolina, and North Carolina
Application: Proposal
Deadline: None
Contact: Charles A. Bundy, President

• •

The Fullerton Foundation, Inc.
P.O. Box 1146
Gaffney, SC 29342
(803) 489-6678

Description: Funds hospitals, health care, and medical research
$ Given: 34 grants totaling $1,203,000; range, $1,000-$132,900
Areas of Support: South Carolina and North Carolina
Application: Initial approach by letter
Deadline: April 1, August 1
Contact: Walter E. Cavell, Executive Director

Monsanto Fund
800 North Lindbergh Boulevard
St. Louis, Missouri 63167
(314) 694-4596

Description: Funding interests include health services, hospitals, social services, youth, education (science and mathematics), and community funds
$ Given: Grants totaling $8,285,748; range, $100-$1,112,000
Areas of Support: Alabama, California, Florida, Georgia, Idaho, Illinois, Massachusetts, Michigan, Missouri, New Jersey, North Carolina, Ohio, South Carolina, Texas, and West Virginia
Application: Proposal
Deadline: None
Contact: John L. Mason, President

Post and Courier Foundation
134 Columbus Street
Charleston, SC 29403
(803) 577-7111

Description: Areas of support include community development, health services, and cultural programs
$ Given: 98 grants totaling $472,364; range, $50-$76,707
Application: Proposal
Deadline: None
Contact: J.F. Smoak, Foundation Manager

The Self Foundation
P.O. Drawer 1017
Greenwood, SC 29648
(803) 229-2571

Description: Focus on health care and higher education, with some support for cultural programs, youth, and the elderly
$ Given: 28 grants totaling $1,032,817; range, $500-$125,000
Application: Proposal
Deadline: March 1, June 1, September 1, and December 1
Contact: Frank L. Wideman, Jr., Executive Vice President

FLOW-THROUGH FUNDING

• •

TENNESSEE

Christy-Houston Foundation
122 North Spring Street
Murfreesboro, TN 37130
(615) 898-1140

Description: Funds hospitals and health-related projects
$ Given: Five grants totaling $158,245; range, $16,000-$49,860
Application: Application form not required
Deadline: January 31
Contact: James R. Arnhart, Executive Director

Hargis (Estes H. and Florence Parker) Charitable Foundation
317 20th Street North
P.O. Box 370404
Birmingham, AL 35237
(205) 251-2881

Description: Funding for health and youth services
$ Given: 7 grants totaling $395,374; range, $300-$376,075
Areas of Support: Alabama, Tennessee
Application: Initial approach by letter
Deadline: May 1
Contact: Gerald D. Colvin, Jr., Chair

The William B. Stokely, Jr. Foundation
620 Campbell Station Road
Station West
Suite Y
Knoxville, Tennessee 37922
(615) 966-4878

Description: Areas of support include education, health services, and cultural programs
$ Given: 96 grants totaling $415,000; range, $50-$50,000
Application: Initial approach by letter or proposal
Deadline: N/A
Contact: William B. Stokely III, President

Washington Foundation
3815 Cleghorn Avenue
P.O. Box 159057
Nashville, TN 37215
(615) 244-0600

Description: Church of Christ-related organizations in the areas of health and welfare
$ Given: 132 grants totaling $682,450; range, $200-$65,000
Application: Initial approach by letter
Deadline: December 1
Contact: Paul A. Hargis, President

TEXAS

Abell-Hanger Foundation
303 West Wall
Room 615
Midland, TX 79701
(915) 684-6655

Description: Areas of support include education, health services, cultural programs, youth activities, and social welfare agencies
$ Given: 110 grants totaling $3,827,099; range, $1,000-$600,000
Application: Application form required
Deadlines: September 30, January 31, and May 31
Contact: David L. Smith, Manager

Arkla Corporate Giving Program
400 East Capitol Avenue
P.O. Box 751
Little Rock, AR 72203
(501) 377-4610

Description: Funds a wide variety of programs, including health services, mental health, AIDS, child welfare and drug abuse.
$ Given: N/A
Limitations: Giving in major operating areas (Arkansas, California, Kansas, Texas, Oklahoma, and Mississippi)
Application: Initial approach by letter
Deadline: None
Contact: James L. Rutherford III, Senior Vice President (Little Rock, Arkansas area) or Hugh H. McCastlain (Shreveport, Louisiana area)

The Cain (Effie and Wofford) Foundation
6116 North Central Expressway
Suite 909-LB65
Dallas, TX 75206
(214) 361-4201

Description: Funding interests include religious organizations, medical services and research, including cancer counseling, and education
$ Given: 56 grants totaling $1,615,230; range, $500-$500,000
Application: Application form required
Deadline: August 31
Contact: Harvey L. Walker, Executive Director

Amon G. Carter Foundation
1212 North CarolinaNB Center
P.O. Box 1036
Fort Worth, TX 76101
(817) 332-2783

Description: Funds arts, health care, education, programs for the aged, and youth agencies
$ Given: 115 grants totaling $8,532,113; range, $500-$3,918,902
Application: Initial approach by letter
Deadline: None
Contact: Bob J. Crowe, Executive Director

FLOW-THROUGH FUNDING

. . . .

Dodge Jones Foundation
P.O. Box 176
Abilene, TX 79604
(915) 673-6429

Description: Areas of support include education, the arts, health, community funds, and youth services
$ Given: 94 grants totaling $2,465,387; range, $100-$500,000
Application: Initial approach by letter
Deadline: None
Contact: Lawrence E. Gill, Vice President, Grants Administration

The Fasken Foundation
500 West Texas Avenue
Suite 1160
Midland, TX 79701
(915) 683-5401

Description: Funding interests include health and social services (including hospices and programs for alcoholism),and education
$ Given: 72 grants totaling $1,028,066; range, $1,000-$105,000
Application: Initial approach by letter
Deadline: December or July
Contact: B.L. Jones, Executive Director

The Favrot Fund
909 Wirt Road
No. 101
Houston, TX 77024
(713) 956-4009

Description: Focus on community-based programs directed toward health, the needy, and the arts
$ Given: 24 grants totaling $310,000; range, $2,000-$25,000
Areas of Support: Texas, California, New York, and Washington, DC
Application: Initial approach by letter
Deadline: None
Contact: Mrs. Carol Parker

The Fondren Foundation
Texas Commerce Tower
Trust Dept., 7th Floor
P.O. Box 2558
Houston, TX 77252
(713) 236-4403

Description: Areas of support include education, health, social service and youth agencies, and cultural organizations
$ Given: 63 grants totaling $3,201,750; range, $1,000-$500,000
Application: Initial approach by letter
Deadline: None
Contact: Melanie A. Boone, Assistant Secretary

The Frees Foundation
5373 West Alabama
Suite 404
Houston, TX 77056
(713) 623-0515

Description: Emphasis on community organizations in Texas and the Republic of Mexico; support includes hospitals and health services
$ Given: 13 grants totaling $153,571; range, $300-$100,000
Application: Proposal
Deadline: None
Contact: Nancy Frees Rosser, Director

The Green Foundation
3300 First City Center
Dallas, TX 75201
(214) 969-1700

Description: Areas of support include hospitals and medical service, cultural programs, education, and a community fund
$ Given: 26 grants totaling $482,150; range, $250-$150,000
Application: Application form not required
Deadline: None
Contact: William E. Collins, Trustee

The Hamman (George and Mary Josephine) Foundation
910 Travis Street
No. 1438
Houston, TX 77002
(713) 658-8345

Description: Funding interests include medical treatment, hospital contruction, education, and social service
$ Given: Grants totaling $637,400; range, $500-$65,000
Application: Initial approach by letter
Deadline: None
Contact: Stephen I. Gelsey, Administrator

Hawn Foundation
1540 Republic Bank Building
Dallas, TX 75201
(214) 220-2828

Description: Areas of support include health service, medical research, education, and cultural programs
$ Given: 41 grants totaling $782,000; range, $500-$250,000
Application: Initial approach by letter
Deadline: None
Contact: E.S. Blythe, Secretary-Treasurer

FLOW-THROUGH FUNDING

. . . .

Hoblitzelle Foundation
1410 Tower 1
NCNB Center
Dallas, TX 75201
(214) 979-0321

Description: Funds education, hospitals and health services, cultural programs, and community development
$ Given: 59 grants totaling $3,289,518; range, $200-$300,000
Application: Initial approach by letter
Deadline: April 15, August 15, December 15
Contact: Paul W. Harris, Executive Vice President

Keebler Company Foundation
One Hollow Tree Lane
Elmhurst, IL 60126
(312) 833-2900

Description: Funding interests include minority programs, health and human services, and education
$ Given: 239 grants totaling $359,987; range, $10-$34,180
Areas of Support: Illinois, Colorado, Indiana, Michigan, Minnesota, North Carolina, Pennsylvania, Texas
Application: Initial approach by letter
Deadline: None
Contact: A.G. Bland, Treasurer

Oliver Dewey Mayor Foundation
c/o AmeriTrust Texas, N.A.
P.O. Box 1088
Sherman, TX 75091
(214) 868-0819

Description: Areas of support include community development, health and social services, education, and youth
$ Given: Grants totaling $278,581
Application: Proposal
Deadline: None
Contact: Philip McKenzie, Trust Officer, AmeriTrust Texas, N.A.

Monsanto Fund
800 North Lindbergh Boulevard
St. Louis, Missouri 63167
(314) 694-4596

Description: Funding interests include health services, hospitals, social services, youth, education (science and mathematics), and community funds
$ Given: Grants totaling $8,285,748; range, $100-$1,112,000
Areas of Support: Alabama, California, Florida, Georgia, Idaho, Illinois, Massachusetts, Michigan, Missouri, New Jersey, North Carolina, Ohio, South Carolina, Texas, and West Virginia
Application: Proposal
Deadline: None
Contact: John L. Mason, President

The Moody Foundation
704 Moody National Bank
Building
Galveston, TX 77550
(409) 763-5333

Description: Funding interests include health services
(including pediatric cardiology), education, and community and social services
$ Given: 79 grants totaling $15,460,064; average range,
$10,000-$150,000
Application: Initial approach by letter or telephone
Deadline: Six weeks prior to quarterly board meetings
Contact: Peter M. Moore, Grants Officer

Dora Roberts Foundation
c/o Texas American Bridge
Bank/Fort Worth
P.O. Box 2050
Fort Worth, TX 76113
(817) 884-4442

Description: Areas of support include education, health
services and hospitals, Protestant church support, and
youth agencies
$ Given: Grants totaling $874,294; range, $780-$230,000
Application: Proposal
Deadline: September 30
Contact: Rick Piersall, Vice President and Trust Officer

Semmes Foundation
800 Navarro
Suite 210
San Antonio, TX 78205
(512) 225-0887

Description: Funds education, health services, the arts
and museums
$ Given: 29 grants totaling $349,948; range, $100-
$151,150
Application: Initial approach by letter
Deadline: None
Contact: Thomas R. Semmes, President

T.L.L. Temple Foundation
109 Temple Boulecard
Lufkin, TX 75901
(409) 639-5197

Description: Areas of support include education, health
services, and community and social services
$ Given: 178 grants totaling $10,009,877; range, $1,000-
$1,250,000
Application: Initial approach by letter
Deadline: None
Contact: Ward R. Burke, Executive Secretary

FLOW-THROUGH FUNDING

Turner Charitable Foundation
811 Rusk Street
Suite 205
Houston, TX 77002
(713) 237-1117

Description: Funding interests include education, hospitals and health services, Catholic, Protestant, and Jewish church support, social service and youth agencies, and arts and cultural programs
$ Given: 57 grants totaling $426,100; range, $100-$75,000
Application: Initial approach by letter
Deadline: March 15
Contact: Eyvonne Moser, Assistant Secretary

The Vale-Asche Foundation
910 River Oaks Bank Building
2001 Kirby Drive
Suite 910
Houston, TX 77019
(713) 520-7334

Description: Funds health care, medical research, aid to the aged and handicapped, and child welfare
$ Given: 19 grants totaling $225,129; range, $1,000-$30,000
Application: Initial approach by letter
Deadline: None
Contact: Mrs. Vale Asche Akerman, President

Crystelle Waggoner Charitable Trust
c/o Texas National Bank
P.O. Box 1317
Fort Worth, TX 76101
(817) 390-6114

Description: Areas of support include health services and associations, arts and cultural programs, and social services
$ Given: 55 grants totaling $286,224; range, $50-$37,000
Application: Initial approach by letter
Deadline: March 31, June 30, September 30, December 31
Contact: Darlene Mann, Vice President, North CarolinaNB Texas National Bank

Lola Wright Foundation, Inc.
P.O. Box 1138
Georgetown, TX 78627
(512) 255-3067

Description: Focus on social service, health and hospitals, the aged, cultural programs, and community funds
$ Given: Grants totaling $564,884; average range, $1,500-$25,000
Application: Initial approach by letter
Deadline: None
Contact: N/A

UTAH

The Dumke (Dr. Ezekial R. and Edna Wattis) Foundation
600 Crandall Building
10 West First South
Salt Lake City, UT 84101
(801) 363-7863

Description: Funds education, medical and hospital services, youth agencies, and cultural programs
$ Given: 27 grants totaling $262,113; range, $1,000-$40,000
Areas of Support: Utah and Illinois
Application: Application form required
Deadline: February 1, July 1
Contact: Max B. Lewis, Secretary

Willard L. Eccles Charitable Foundation
P.O. Box 45385
Salt Lake City, UT 84145
(801) 532-1500

Description: Areas of support include
$ Given: 15 grants totaling $1,000,383; range, $2,000-$235,000
Application: Initial approach by letter
Deadline: Month preceeding board meetings (board meets in March, June, and October)
Contact: Clark P. Giles, Secretary

FHP Foundation
401 East Ocean Boulevard
Suite 206
Long Beach, CA 90802
(310) 590-8655

Description: Funds direct delivery of health care services, including education programs, programs for the elderly and chronically ill, and primary care projects in underserved areas.
$ Given: 17 grants totaling $773,064; range, $2,900-$89,000
Areas of Support: Giving in southern California, Utah, New Mexico, Arizona
Application: Initial approach by letter
Deadline: February 15, May 15, August 15, and Nov. 15
Contact: Sandra Lund Gavin, Executive Director

Questar Corporate Giving Program
180 East First South Street
P.O. Box 11150
Salt Lake City, UT 84147
(801) 534-5435

Description: Funding interests include the aged, medical and health services, education, the disadvantaged, and arts and culture
$ Given: Grants totaling $330,000
Application: Initial approach by letter
Deadline: None
Contact: Janice Bates, Director of Community Affairs

FLOW-THROUGH FUNDING

. . . .

VERMONT

Agnes M. Lindsay Trust
45 Market Street
Manchester, NH 03101
(603) 669-4140

Description: Funding interests include health services, higher education, services for the handicapped, and welfare institutions
$ Given: 191 grants totaling $863,771; average range, $1,000-$10,000
Areas of Support: Maine, Massachusetts, New Hampshire, and Vermont
Application: Proposal
Deadline: None
Contact: Robert L. Chiesa, Trustee

National Life Insurance Corporate Contributions Program
National Life Drive
Montpelier, VT 05604
(802) 229-3333

Description: Areas of support include health, education, arts and culture, and civic and community affairs
$ Given: 150 grants totaling $161,000; range, $50-$15,000
Application: Initial approach by letter
Deadline: None
Contact: Jane W. Robb, Communications Associate

VIRGINIA

Cartledge Charitable Foundation, Inc.
P.O. Box 12528
Roanoke, VA 24026
(703) 343-1701

Description: Funding interests include education, health services, and youth organizations
$ Given: 117 grants totaling $233,734; range, $25-$30,000
Application: Initial approach by letter
Deadline: None
Contact: N/A

Massey Foundation
P.O. Box 26765
Richmond, VA 23261
(804) 788-1800

Description: Areas of support include education, health services and hospitals, social services, and cultural programs
$ Given: 76 grants totaling $1,367,250; range, $1,000-$210,000
Application: Initial approach by letter
Deadline: None
Contact: William E. Massey, Jr., President

Universal Leaf Foundation
P.O. Box 25099
Richmond, VA 23260
(804) 359-9311

Description: Funding interests include education, health, medical research, youth agencies, and the arts
$ Given: 175 grants totaling $354,176; range, $75-$31,000
Application: Initial approach by letter
Deadline: None
Contact: Nancy G. Powell, Manager of Corporate Relations

Wheat Foundation
707 East Main Street
Richmond, VA 23219
(804) 649-2311

Description: Funds higher and secondary education, cultural programs, health services, and hospitals
$ Given: 160 grants totaling $340,000; range, $500-$100,000
Areas of Support: Virginia, Washington, DC, Delaware, Georgia, Maryland, North Carolina, Pennsylvania, and West Virginia
Application: Initial approach by letter or telephone
Deadline: None
Contact: William V. Daniel, Treasurer and Trustee

WASHINGTON

The William G. Gilmore Foundation
120 Montgomery Street
Suite 1880
San Francisco, CA 94104
(415) 546-1400

Description: Funds community-based organization, including family and social services, health services, and AIDS programs
$ Given: 132 grants totaling $766,345; range, $200-$50,000
Areas of Support: Giving in northern California, Oregon, and Washington
Application: Initial approach by mail
Deadlines: May 1, November 1
Contact: Faye Wilson, Secretary

FLOW-THROUGH FUNDING

. . . .

Glaser Foundation, Inc.
P.O. Box N
Edmonds, WA 98020

Description: Areas of support include direct-line service health agencies, drug abuse programs, the aged, the indigent, youth, and the handicapped
$ Given: 62 grants totaling $236,772; range, $50-$10,245
Application: Application form required; Initial approach by letter
Deadline: None
Contact: R.W. Carlstrom, Executive Director

Joshua Green Foundation, Inc.
1414 Fourth Avenue
P.O. Box 720
Seattle, WA 98111
(206) 344-2285

Description: Funding interests include education, health services and agencies, community funds, and church support
$ Given: 60 grants totaling $269,423; range, $200-$80,000
Application: Proposal
Deadline: None
Contact: N/A

George Frederick Jewett Foundation
One Maritime Plaza
Suite 990
San Francisco, CA 94111
(415) 421-1351

Description: Interests include health care and medical research and services
$ Given: 134 grants totaling $953,597; range, $500-$25,000
Areas of Support: San Francisco, California; eastern Washington; northern Idaho
Application: Initial approach by letter
Deadlines: February 15, May 15, August 15, and November 1
Contact: Theresa A. Mullen, Program Director

Lockwood (Byron W. and Alice L.) Foundation
8121 S.E. 44th Street
Mercer Island, WA 98040
(206) 232-1881

Description: Funds health, culture, education, and youth and social service organizations
$ Given: 38 grants totaling $418,800; range, $500-$100,000
Application: Initial approach by letter
Deadline: N/A
Contact: Sally Easterbrook

• •

Meyer Memorial Trust
1515 S.W. Fifth Avenue
Suite 500
Portland, OR 97201
(503) 228-5512

Description: General purpose grants in Oregon for education, health and social welfare, arts and humanities; special program grants for Aging and Independence and Support for Children at Risk in Oregon, Alaska, Idaho, Montana, and Washington; operates a Small Grants Program (500-$8,000) for small projects in Oregon
$ Given: 209 grants totaling $11,953,746; range, $500-$2,000,000
Application: Application form required
Deadline: April 1, October 1 for Aging and Independence; July 15, October 15 for Small Grants Program; no deadline for general purpose grants
Contact: Charles S. Rooks, Executive Director

Puget Sound Power and Light Corporate Giving Program
P.O. Box 97034
Bellevue, WA 98009
(206) 462-3799

Description: Areas of support include education, health services, hospitals, arts and humanities, and environmental programs
$ Given: 79 grants totaling $597,101; range, $50-$25,000
Application: Initial approach by short letter
Deadline: Late summer and early fall
Contact: Neil L. McReynolds, Senior Vice President, Corporate Relations

Spokane Inland Northwest Community Foundation
400 Paulsen Center
West 421 Riverside Avenue
Spokane, WA 99201
(509) 624-2606

Description: Funding interests include the elderly, music and the arts, social and health services, and education
$ Given: 440 grants totaling $738,429; average grant, $1,500
Areas of Support: The inland northwest (Washington and Idaho)
Application: Initial approach by letter
Deadlines: October 1 (Spokane, Washington); November 1 (Pullman and Dayton, Washington); May 1 (northern Idaho); and October 15 (ISC fund)
Contact: Jeanne L. Ager, Executive Director

Washington Mutual Savings Bank Foundation
c/o Washington Mutual Tower
P.O. Box 834, 1201 Third Ave.
Seattle, WA 98111
(206) 461-4663

Description: Areas of support include health and welfare, education, cultural enhancement, and civic betterment
$ Given: 176 grants totaling $593,113; range, $500-$40,000
Application: Application form required
Deadline: March 31, June 30, September 31, December 31
Contact: Greg Tuke, Program Administrator

FLOW-THROUGH FUNDING

• • • • • • • • • • • • • • • • • • • •

WEST VIRGINIA

Clay Foundation
1426 Kanawha Boulevard
East
Charleston, WV 25301
(304) 344-8656

Description: Funds aging, health care, vocational education, and disadvantaged youth
$ Given: 17 grants totaling $905,965; range, $2,000-$300,000
Application: Proposal
Deadline: Write for information
Contact: Betsy B. VonBlond, Executive Director

WISCONSIN

Badger Meter Foundation
4545 West Brown Deer
Road
Milwaukee, WI 53223
(414) 355-0400

Description: Areas of support include health care, education, community funds, the disabled, and the arts
$ Given: 119 grants totaling $286,200; range, $25-$20,000
Application: Initial approach by letter
Deadline: August 31
Contact: Mary George, Secretary

Chapman Foundation
777 East Wisconsin Avenue
Suite 3090
Milwaukee, WI 53202
(414) 276-6955

Description: Funds education, health services, conservation, and culture
$ Given: 48 grants totaling $246,280; range, $100-$100,000
Application: Applications not accepted; giving to preselected organizations
Deadline: N/A
Contact: George M. Chester, President

John Deere Foundation
John Deere Road
Moline, IL 61265
(309) 765-4137

Description: Areas of support include health services, community funds, youth agencies, and education
$ Given: Grants totaling $3,707,974; range, $300-$539,000
Areas of Support: Iowa, Illinois, Wisconsin
Application: Initial approach by letter
Deadline: None
Contact: Donald R. Morgenthaler, President

The Donaldson Foundation
c/o Donaldson Company, Inc.
P.O. Box 1299
Minneapolis, MN 55440
(612) 887-3010

Description: Funding interests include health services, environmental protection, and higher education
$ Given: 98 grants totaling $338,875; range, $300-$38,400
Areas of Support: Illinois, Indiana, Iowa, Kentucky, Minnesota, Missouri, and Wisconsin
Application: Initial approach by letter
Deadline: May 1, August 1
Contact: Raymond Vodovnik, Secretary

Fannie Mae Foundation
3900 Wisconsin Avenue, N.W.
Washington, DC 20016
(202) 752-6500

Description: Funding interests include housing and community development, and health and social concerns
$ Given: 300 grants totaling $1,151,567; range, $100-$50,000
Areas of Support: Washington, DC; Pasadena, California; Atlanta, Georgia; Chicago, Illinois; and Philadelphia, PA
Application: Proposal
Deadline: None
Contact: Harriet M. Ivey, Executive Director

Fort Howard Foundation, Inc.
P.O. Box 11325
Green Bay, WI 54307
(414) 435-8821

Description: Areas of support include education, health care facilities, cultural programs, and social service and youth agencies
$ Given: Six grants totaling $726,652; range, $13,700-$150,000
Areas of Support: Green Bay, Wisconsin; Muskogee, Oklahoma; and Effingham County, Georgia
Application: The foundation is not presently making any new funding commitments
Contact: Bruce W. Nagel, Executive Director

Madison Community Foundation
615 East Washington Avenue
Madison, WI 53703
(608) 255-0503

Description: Funding interests include health and human services, youth, art and culture, education, and econominc development
$ Given: 48 grants totaling $356,826
Application: Initial approach by letter
Deadlines: February 1 for letter of intent; March 15 for proposal
Contact: Jane Taylor Coleman, Executive Director

FLOW-THROUGH FUNDING

Faye McBeath Foundation
1020 North Broadway
Milwaukee, WI 53202
(414) 272-2626

Description: Areas of support include homes and care for the elderly, medical, nursing, and hospital care for the sick, and child welfare
$ Given: 53 grants totaling $1,414,337; range, $15,000-$75,000
Application: Initial approach by letter
Deadlines: One month prior to board meetings (board meets bimonthly)
Contact: Sarah M. Dean, Executive Director

Milwaukee Foundation
1020 North Broadway
Milwaukee, WI 53202
(414) 272-5805

Description: Areas of support include health care and hospitals, educational institutions, social services, and arts and cultural programs
$ Given: 429 rants totaling $4,004,551; range, $100-$175,000
Application: Initial approach by letter, proposal, or telephone
Deadlines: January 2, March 1, June 18, September 17, and December 17
Contact: David M.G. Huntington, Executive Director

Time Insurance Foundation
515 West Wells Street
Milwaukee, WI 53203

Description: Funds community service, with emphasis on health care services, education, and the arts
$ Given: 156 grants totaling $294,484; range, $50-$100,000
Application: Initial approach by letter requesting guidelines
Deadline: None
Contact: John E. Krick, President

State and Regional Government Grants

· ·

This chapter lists state and regional government agencies that can be of assistance in your search for funding. For the most part, these agencies represent a local level of access to federal funding programs and organizations. For example, the Department of Health and Human Services (DHHS) has several regional offices; individuals or groups applying for funds from a DHHS national program (such as "Community Health Centers") must make their applications through their regional offices. Because each government agency administers several different funding programs, and because monies available vary from year to year, the state-by-state information provided here is, for the most part, listed in a generic form. For details about the federal funding programs administered through these regional offices, please refer to the next chapter, "Federal Grants."

Also included in this chapter are Native and Indian Health Service grants, which provide funding for American Indians and Native Alaskans. These grants are administered through local offices serving their immediate areas. Money is awarded directly to federally-recognized tribes or tribal organizations which, in turn, use the money to provide health-related services to tribal members who need them.

The price of health care is a major and growing worry for federal, state and local governments, which must devote a rising share of their strained budgets to paying for health care. More than forty percent of the nation's health bills are now covered by government programs. Despite this, federal monies still exist.

STATE AND REGIONAL GOVERNMENT GRANTS

Before you call the contact person in your state, I suggest that you make a list of what it is you need monies for (i.e., hospital bills, long-term care costs, loss of income replacement). Ask yourself such questions as, are there demonstrated financial needs on the part of the patient or the patient's family? In this fashion, you can address every issue leading to support and aid in one telephone call — by being able to describe precisely the kinds of funding for which you may be eligible.

When you call, ask this: "What types of funding pro- grams do you provide?" If the response does not include a program that meets your particular needs, ask more specific questions. If the agency you call does not offer a program to meet your needs, someone there may be able to direct you to an agency that does. If the agency publishes materials describing its funding programs, request that these be mailed to you, along with an application. Also make sure to find out if there is a deadline coming up, so that you will be able to return any applications by that time.

· ·

ALABAMA

Department of Health and Human Services, Region IV Office
101 Marietta Tower
Suite 1515
Atlanta, GA 30323
(404) 331-2442

Contact: Earl Forsythe

Department of Labor
Employment and Training Administration, Region IV Office
1371 Peachtree Street, NE
Room 400
Atlanta, GA 30367
(404) 347-4411

Contact: Daniel L. Lowry

ALASKA

Department of Health and Human Services, Region X Office
2201 Sixth Avenue
RX-01
Seattle, WA 98121
(206) 553-0420

Contact: Elizabeth G. Healy

Department of Labor
Employment and Training Administration, Region X Office
Federal Office Building
909 First Avenue
Room 1136
Seattle, WA 98174
(206) 442-7700

Contact: Armando Quriz

STATE AND REGIONAL GOVERNMENT GRANTS

. . . .

Alaska Area Native Health Service
P.O. Box 107741
Anchorage, AK 99510
(907) 257-1153

Program: Indian Health Service — Health Management Development Program (Federal program 93.228)
Description: Funding for American Indian/Native Alaskan projects designed to provide a full range of curative, preventive and rehabilitative health services. Assistance to federally-recognized tribes and tribal organizations. Designed to increase the capability of American Indians and Native Alaskans to manage their own health programs.
Restrictions: Only federally-recognized tribes and tribal organizations may apply
$ Given: Range of $6,250 - $6.3 million per project; average award is $62,693 (national figures)
Number of Awards: Approximately 100 awards made annually nationwide
Application Information: Contact local Health Service office for standard application forms
Deadline: Submit application 90 days prior to proposed project start date
National Contacts: Kay Carpentier, grants management contact, (301) 443-5204; or B. Bowman, program contact, (301) 443-6840
Local Contact: Gerald Ivey

ARIZONA

Department of Health and Human Services, Region IX Office
Federal Office Building
50 United Nations Plaza
Room 431
San Francisco, CA 94102
(415) 556-1961

Contact: Emory Lee

Department of Labor
Employment and Training Administration, Region IX Office
71 Stevenson Street
Room 830
PO Box 3767
San Francisco, CA 94105
(415) 744-6650

Contact: Don A. Balcer

• • • • • • • • • • • • • • • • • • •

Phoenix Area Indian Health Service
3738 North 16th Street
Suite A
Phoenix, AZ 85016-5981
(602) 241-2052
Contact: Don J. Davis
and
Navajo Area Indian Health Service
P.O. Box G
Window Rock, AZ 86515
(602) 871-5811
and
Tucson Area Indian Health Service
7900 South J. Stock Road
Tucson, AZ 85746-9352
(602) 629-6600
Contact: Eleanore Robertson

Program: Indian Health Service — Health Management Development Program (Federal program 93.228)
Description: Funding for American Indian projects designed to provide a full range of curative, preventive and rehabilitative health services. Assistance to federally-recognized tribes and tribal organizations. Designed to increase the capability of American Indians to manage their own health programs.
Restrictions: Only federally-recognized tribes and tribal organizations may apply
$ Given: Range of $6,250 - $6.3 million per project; average award is $62,693 (national figures)
Number of Awards: Approximately 100 awards made annually nationwide
Application Information: Contact local Health Service office for standard application forms
Deadline: Submit application 90 days prior to proposed project start date
National Contacts: Kay Carpentier, grants management contact, (301) 443-5204; or B. Bowman, program contact, (301) 443-6840

STATE AND REGIONAL GOVERNMENT GRANTS

. . . .

ARKANSAS

Department of Health and Human Services, Region VI Office
1200 Main Tower Building
Room 1100
Dallas, TX 75202
(214) 767-3301

Contact: J.B. Keith

Department of Labor
Employment and Training Administration, Region VI Office
525 Griffin Street
Room 317
Dallas, TX 75202
(214) 767-8263

Contact: Floyd E. Edwards

CALIFORNIA

Department of Health and Human Services, Region IX Office
Federal Office Building
50 United Nations Plaza
Room 431
San Francisco, CA 94102
(415) 556-1961

Contact: Emory Lee

Department of Labor
Employment and Training Administration, Region IX Office
71 Stevenson Street
Room 830
P.O. Box 3767
San Francisco, CA 94105
(415) 744-6650

Contact: Don A. Balcer

. . . .

California Area Indian Health Service
2999 Fulton Avenue
Sacramento, CA 95821
(916) 978-4202

Program: Indian Health Service — Health Management Development Program (Federal program 93.228)
Description: Funding for American Indian projects designed to provide a full range of curative, preventive and rehabilitative health services. Assistance to federally-recognized tribes and tribal organizations. Designed to increase the capability of American Indians to manage their own health programs.
Restrictions: Only federally-recognized tribes and tribal organizations may apply
$ Given: Range of $6,250 - $6.3 million per project; average award is $62,693 (national figures)
Number of Awards: Approximately 100 awards made annually nationwide
Application Information: Contact local Health Service office for standard application forms
Deadline: Submit application 90 days prior to proposed project start date
National Contacts: Kay Carpenter, grants management contact, (301) 443-5204; or B. Bowman, program contact, (301) 443-6840
Local Contact: T.J. Harwood

COLORADO

Department of Health and Human Services, Region VIII Office
Federal Building
Room 1185
1961 Stout Street
Denver, CO 80294-3538
(303) 844-3372

Contact: Paul Denham

Department of Labor
Employment and Training Administration, Region VIII Office
Federal Building
Room 1640
1961 Stout Street
Denver, CO 80294
(303) 844-4477

Contact: Luis Sepulveda

STATE AND REGIONAL GOVERNMENT GRANTS

· ·

CONNECTICUT

Department of Health and Human Services, Region I Office
John F. Kennedy Federal Building
Room 2411
Government Center
Boston, MA 02203
(617) 565-1500

Contact: Maureen Osolnik

Department of Labor
Employment and Training Administration, Region I Office
John F. Kennedy Federal Building
Room 1707
Government Center
Boston, MA 02203
(617) 565-3630

Contact: Robert J. Semler

DELAWARE

Department of Health and Human Services, Region III Office
3535 Market Street
Room 11480
Gateway Building
Philadelphia, PA 19104
MAIL ADDRESS: P.O. Box 13716, Mail Stop No. 1, Philadelphia, PA 19101
(215) 596-6492

Contact: James Mengel

Department of Labor
Employment and Training Administration, Region III Office
P.O. Box 8796
Philadelphia, PA 19101
(215) 596-6336

Contact: William J. Haltigan

. . . .

DISTRICT OF COLUMBIA

Department of Health and Human Services, Region III Office
3535 Market Street
Room 11480
Gateway Building
Philadelphia, PA 19104
MAIL ADDRESS: P.O. Box 13716, Mail Stop No. 1, Philadelphia, PA 19101
(215) 596-6492

Contact: James Mengel

Department of Labor
Employment and Training Administration, Region III Office
P.O. Box 8796
Philadelphia, PA 19101
(215) 596-6336

Contact: William J. Haltigan

FLORIDA

Department of Health and Human Services, Region IV Office
101 Marietta Tower
Suite 1515
Atlanta, GA 30323
(404) 331-2442

Contact: Earl Forsythe

Department of Labor
Employment and Training Administration, Region IV Office
1371 Peachtree Street, NE
Room 400
Atlanta, GA 30367
(404) 347-4411

Contact: Daniel L. Lowry

STATE AND REGIONAL GOVERNMENT GRANTS

. . . .

GEORGIA

Department of Health and Human Services, Region IV Office
101 Marietta Tower
Suite 1515
Atlanta, GA 30323
(404) 331-2442

Contact: Earl Forsythe

Department of Labor
Employment and Training Administration, Region IV Office
1371 Peachtree Street, NE
Room 400
Atlanta, GA 30367
(404) 347-4411

Contact: Daniel L. Lowry

HAWAII

Department of Health and Human Services, Region IX Office
Federal Office Building
50 United Nations Plaza
Room 431
San Francisco, CA 94102
(415) 556-1961

Contact: Emory Lee

Department of Labor
Employment and Training Administration, Region IX Office
71 Stevenson Street
Room 830
P.O. Box 3767
San Francisco, CA 94105
(415) 744-6650

Contact: Don A. Balcer

• • • • • • • • • • • • • • • • • • • •

IDAHO

Department of Health and Human Services, Region X Office
2201 Sixth Avenue
RX-01
Seattle, WA 98121
(206) 553-0420

Contact: Elizabeth G. Healy

Department of Labor
Employment and Training Administration, Region X Office
Federal Office Building
909 First Avenue
Room 1136
Seattle, WA 98174
(206) 442-7700

Contact: Armando Quriz

ILLINOIS

Department of Health and Human Services, Region V Office
105 West Adams
23rd Floor
Chicago, IL 60603
(312) 353-5132

Contact: Hiroshi Kanno

Department of Labor
Employment and Training Administration, Region V Office
230 S. Dearborn Street
Room 628
Chicago, IL 60604
(312) 353-0313

Contact: Joseph Juarez

STATE AND REGIONAL GOVERNMENT GRANTS

INDIANA

Department of Health and Human Services, Region V Office
105 West Adams
23rd Floor
Chicago, IL 60603
(312) 353-5132

Contact: Hiroshi Kanno

Department of Labor
Employment and Training Administration, Region V Office
230 S. Dearborn Street
Room 628
Chicago, IL 60604
(312) 353-0313

Contact: Joseph Juarez

IOWA

Department of Health and Human Services, Region VII Office
601 East 12th Street
Room 210
Kansas City, MO 64106
(816) 426-2821

Contact: Barbara Gumminger

Department of Labor
Employment and Training Administration, Region VII Office
Federal Building
Room 700
911 Walnut Street
Kansas City, MO 64106
(816) 426-3796

Contact: Grace A. Kilbane

• • • • • • • • • • • • • • • • • • • •

KANSAS

Department of Health and Human Services, Region VII Office
601 East 12th Street
Room 210
Kansas City, MO 64106
(816) 426-2821

Contact: Barbara Gumminger

Department of Labor
Employment and Training Administration, Region VII Office
Federal Building
Room 700
911 Walnut Street
Kansas City, MO 64106
(816) 426-3796

Contact: Grace A. Kilbane

KENTUCKY

Department of Health and Human Services, Region IV Office
101 Marietta Tower
Suite 1515
Atlanta, GA 30323
(404) 331-2442

Contact: Earl Forsythe

Department of Labor
Employment and Training Administration, Region IV Office
1371 Peachtree Street, NE
Room 400
Atlanta, GA 30367
(404) 347-4411

Contact: Daniel L. Lowry

STATE AND REGIONAL GOVERNMENT GRANTS

· ·

LOUISIANA

Department of Health and Human Services, Region VI Office
1200 Main Tower Building
Room 1100
Dallas, TX 75202
(214) 767-3301

Contact: J.B. Keith

Department of Labor
Employment and Training Administration, Region VI Office
525 Griffin Street
Room 317
Dallas, TX 75202
(214) 767-8263

Contact: Floyd E. Edwards

MAINE

Department of Health and Human Services, Region I Office
John F. Kennedy Federal Building
Room 2411
Government Center
Boston, MA 02203
(617) 565-1500

Contact: Maureen Osolnik

Department of Labor
Employment and Training Administration, Region I Office
John F. Kennedy Federal Building
Room 1707
Government Center
Boston, MA 02203
(617) 565-3630

Contact: Robert J. Semler

. . . .

MARYLAND

Department of Health and Human Services, Region III Office
3535 Market Street
Room 11480
Gateway Building
Philadelphia, PA 19104
MAIL ADDRESS: P.O. Box 13716, Mail Stop No. 1, Philadelphia, PA 19101
(215) 596-6492

Contact: James Mengel

Department of Labor
Employment and Training Administration, Region III Office
P.O. Box 8796
Philadelphia, PA 19101
(215) 596-6336

Contact: William J. Haltigan

MASSACHUSETTS

Department of Health and Human Services, Region I Office
John F. Kennedy Federal Building
Room 2411
Government Center
Boston, MA 02203
(617) 565-1500

Contact: Maureen Osolnik

Department of Labor
Employment and Training Administration, Region I Office
John F. Kennedy Federal Building
Room 1707
Government Center
Boston, MA 02203
(617) 565-3630

Contact: Robert J. Semler

STATE AND REGIONAL GOVERNMENT GRANTS

. . . .

MICHIGAN

Department of Health and Human Services, Region V Office
105 West Adams
23rd Floor
Chicago, IL 60603
(312) 353-5132

Contact: Hiroshi Kanno

Department of Labor
Employment and Training Administration, Region V Office
230 S. Dearborn Street
Room 628
Chicago, IL 60604
(312) 353-0313

Contact: Joseph Juarez

MINNESOTA

Department of Health and Human Services, Region V Office
105 West Adams
23rd Floor
Chicago, IL 60603
(312) 353-5132

Contact: Hiroshi Kanno

Department of Labor
Employment and Training Administration, Region V Office
230 S. Dearborn Street
Room 628
Chicago, IL 60604
(312) 353-0313

Contact: Joseph Juarez

• • • • • • • • • • • • • • • • • •

Bemidji Area Indian Health Service
203 Federal Building
Bemidji, MN 56601
(218) 751-7701

Program: Indian Health Service — Health Management Development Program (Federal program 93.228)
Description: Funding for American Indian projects designed to provide a full range of curative, preventive and rehabilitative health services. Assistance to federally-recognized tribes and tribal organizations. Designed to increase the capability of American Indians to manage their own health programs.
Restrictions: Only federally-recognized tribes and tribal organizations may apply
$ Given: Range of $6,250 - $6.3 million per project; average award is $62,693 (national figures)
Number of Awards: Approximately 100 awards made annually nationwide
Application Information: Contact local Health Service office for standard application forms
Deadline: Submit application 90 days prior to proposed project start date
National Contacts: Kay Carpentier, grants management contact, (301) 443-5204; or B. Bowman, program contact, (301) 443-6840
Local Contact: Dr. Kathleen Annette, Director

MISSISSIPPI

Department of Health and Human Services, Region IV Office
101 Marietta Tower
Suite 1515
Atlanta, GA 30323
(404) 331-2442

Contact: Earl Forsythe

Department of Labor
Employment and Training Administration, Region IV Office
1371 Peachtree Street, NE
Room 400
Atlanta, GA 30367
(404) 347-4411

Contact: Daniel L. Lowry

STATE AND REGIONAL GOVERNMENT GRANTS

. . . .

MISSOURI

Department of Health and Human Services, Region VII Office
601 East 12th Street
Room 210
Kansas City, MO 64106
(816) 426-2821

Contact: Barbara Gumminger

Department of Labor
Employment and Training Administration, Region VII Office
Federal Building
Room 700
911 Walnut Street
Kansas City, MO 64106
(816) 426-3796

Contact: Grace A. Kilbane

MONTANA

Department of Health and Human Services, Region VIII Office
Federal Building
Room 1185
1961 Stout Street
Denver, CO 80294-3538
(303) 844-3372

Contact: Paul Denham

Department of Labor
Employment and Training Administration, Region VIII Office
Federal Building
Room 1640
1961 Stout Street
Denver, CO 80294
(303) 844-4477

Contact: Luis Sepulveda

. . . .

Billings Area Indian Health Service
711 Central Avenue
P.O. Box 2143
Billings, MT 59103
(406) 657-6403

Program: Indian Health Service — Health Management Development Program (Federal program 93.228)
Description: Funding for American Indian projects designed to provide a full range of curative, preventive and rehabilitative health services. Assistance to federally-recognized tribes and tribal organizations. Designed to increase the capability of American Indians to manage their own health programs.
Restrictions: Only federally-recognized tribes and tribal organizations may apply
$ Given: Range of $6,250 - $6.3 million per project; average award is $62,693 (national figures)
Number of Awards: Approximately 100 awards made annually nationwide
Application Information: Contact local Health Service office for standard application forms
Deadline: Submit application 90 days prior to proposed project start date
National Contacts: Kay Carpentier, grants management contact, (301) 443-5204; or B. Bowman, program contact, (301) 443-6840
Local Contact: Duane L. Jeanotte

NEBRASKA

Department of Health and Human Services, Region VII Office
601 East 12th Street
Room 210
Kansas City, MO 64106
(816) 426-2821

Contact: Barbara Gumminger

Department of Labor
Employment and Training Administration, Region VII Office
Federal Building
Room 700
911 Walnut Street
Kansas City, MO 64106
(816) 426-3796

Contact: Grace A. Kilbane

STATE AND REGIONAL GOVERNMENT GRANTS

· ·

NEVADA

Department of Health and Human Services, Region IX Office
Federal Office Building
50 United Nations Plaza
Room 431
San Francisco, CA 94102
(415) 556-1961

Contact: Emory Lee

Department of Labor
Employment and Training Administration, Region IX Office
71 Stevenson Street
Room 830
P.O. Box 3767
San Francisco, CA 94105
(415) 744-6650

Contact: Don A. Balcer

NEW HAMPSHIRE

Department of Health and Human Services, Region I Office
John F. Kennedy Federal Building
Room 2411
Government Center
Boston, MA 02203
(617) 565-1500

Contact: Maureen Osolnik

Department of Labor
Employment and Training Administration, Region I Office
John F. Kennedy Federal Building
Room 1707
Government Center
Boston, MA 02203
(617) 565-3630

Contact: Robert J. Semler

. . . .

NEW JERSEY

Department of Health and Human Services, Region II Office
26 Federal Plaza
Room 3835
New York, NY 10278
(212) 264-4600

Contact: Kathleen Harten

Department of Labor
Employment and Training Administration, Region II Office
201 Varick Steet
Room 755
New York, NY 10014
(212) 337-2139

Contact: Thomas E. Hill

NEW MEXICO

Department of Health and Human Services, Region VI Office
1200 Main Tower Building
Room 1100
Dallas, TX 75202
(214) 767-3301

Contact: J.B. Keith

Department of Labor
Employment and Training Administration, Region VI Office
525 Griffin Street
Room 317
Dallas, TX 75202
(214) 767-8263

Contact: Floyd E. Edwards

STATE AND REGIONAL GOVERNMENT GRANTS

. . . .

Albuquerque Area Indian Health Service
Headquarters West Indian Health Service
Federal Office Building and U.S. Courthouse
505 Marquette Avenue, NW
Suite 1502
Albuquerque, NM 87102-2162
(505) 766-2151

Program: Indian Health Service — Health Management Development Program (Federal program 93.228)
Description: Funding for American Indian projects designed to provide a full range of curative, preventive and rehabilitative health services. Assistance to federally-recognized tribes and tribal organizations. Designed to increase the capability of American Indians to manage their own health programs.
Restrictions: Only federally-recognized tribes and tribal organizations may apply
$ Given: Range of $6,250 - $6.3 million per project; average award is $62,693 (national figures)
Number of Awards: Approximately 100 awards made annually nationwide
Application Information: Contact local Health Service office for standard application forms
Deadline: Submit application 90 days prior to proposed project start date
National Contacts: Kay Carpentier, grants management contact, (301) 443-5204; or B. Bowman, program contact, (301) 443-6840
Local Contact: Eleanore Robertson

NEW YORK

Department of Health and Human Services, Region II Office
26 Federal Plaza
Room 3835
New York, NY 10278
(212) 264-4600

Contact: Kathleen Harten

Department of Labor
Employment and Training Administration, Region II Office
201 Varick Steet
Room 755
New York, NY 10014
(212) 337-2139

Contact: Thomas E. Hill

. . . .

NORTH CAROLINA

Department of Health and Human Services, Region IV Office
101 Marietta Tower
Suite 1515
Atlanta, GA 30323
(404) 331-2442

Contact: Earl Forsythe

Department of Labor
Employment and Training Administration, Region IV Office
1371 Peachtree Street, NE
Room 400
Atlanta, GA 30367
(404) 347-4411

Contact: Daniel L. Lowry

NORTH DAKOTA

Department of Health and Human Services, Region VIII Office
Federal Building
Room 1185
1961 Stout Street
Denver, CO 80294-3538
(303) 844-3372

Contact: Paul Denham

Department of Labor
Employment and Training Administration, Region VIII Office
Federal Building
Room 1640
1961 Stout Street
Denver, CO 80294
(303) 844-4477

Contact: Luis Sepulveda

STATE AND REGIONAL GOVERNMENT GRANTS

· ·

OHIO

Department of Health and Human Services, Region V Office
105 West Adams
23rd Floor
Chicago, IL 60603
(312) 353-5132

Contact: Hiroshi Kanno

Department of Labor
Employment and Training Administration, Region V Office
230 S. Dearborn Street
Room 628
Chicago, IL 60604
(312) 353-0313

Contact: Joseph Juarez

OKLAHOMA

Department of Health and Human Services, Region VI Office
1200 Main Tower Building
Room 1100
Dallas, TX 75202
(214) 767-3301

Contact: J.B. Keith

Department of Labor
Employment and Training Administration, Region VI Office
525 Griffin Street
Room 317
Dallas, TX 75202
(214) 767-8263

Contact: Floyd E. Edwards

• • • • • • • • • • • • • • • • • • • •

Oklahoma City Area Indian Health Service
215 Dean A. McGee Street, NW
Oklahoma City, OK 73102-3477
(405) 237-4796

Program: Indian Health Service — Health Management Development Program (Federal program 93.228)
Description: Funding for American Indian projects designed to provide a full range of curative, preventive and rehabilitative health services. Assistance to federally-recognized tribes and tribal organizations. Designed to increase the capability of American Indians to manage their own health programs.
Restrictions: Only federally-recognized tribes and tribal organizations may apply
$ Given: Range of $6,250 - $6.3 million per project; average award is $62,693 (national figures)
Number of Awards: Approximately 100 awards made annually nationwide
Application Information: Contact local Health Service office for standard application forms
Deadline: Submit application 90 days prior to proposed project start date
National Contacts: Kay Carpentier, grants management contact, (301) 443-5204; or B. Bowman, program contact, (301) 443-6840
Local Contact: Dr. Robert Harry, Director

OREGON

Department of Health and Human Services, Region X Office
2201 Sixth Avenue
RX-01
Seattle, WA 98121
(206) 553-0420

Contact: Elizabeth G. Healy

Department of Labor
Employment and Training Administration, Region X Office
Federal Office Building
909 First Avenue
Room 1136
Seattle, WA 98174
(206) 442-7700

Contact: Armando Quriz

STATE AND REGIONAL GOVERNMENT GRANTS

. . . .

Portland Area Indian Health Service
1220 S.W. Third Avenue
Room 476
Portland, OR 97204-2892
(503) 221-2020

Program: Indian Health Service — Health Management Development Program (Federal program 93.228)
Description: Funding for American Indian projects designed to provide a full range of curative, preventive and rehabilitative health services. Assistance to federally-recognized tribes and tribal organizations. Designed to increase the capability of American Indians to manage their own health programs.
Restrictions: Only federally-recognized tribes and tribal organizations may apply
$ Given: Range of $6,250 - $6.3 million per project; average award is $62,693 (national figures)
Number of Awards: Approximately 100 awards made annually nationwide
Application Information: Contact local Health Service office for standard application forms
Deadline: Submit application 90 days prior to proposed project start date
National Contacts: Kay Carpentier, grants management contact, (301) 443-5204; or B. Bowman, program contact, (301) 443-6840
Local Contact: Dr. Terrance Batliner, Director

PENNSYLVANIA

Department of Health and Human Services, Region III Office
3535 Market Street
Room 11480
Gateway Building
Philadelphia, PA 19104
MAIL ADDRESS: P.O. Box 13716, Mail Stop No. 1, Philadelphia, PA 19101
(215) 596-6492

Contact: James Mengel

Department of Labor
Employment and Training Administration, Region III Office
P.O. Box 8796
Philadelphia, PA 19101
(215) 596-6336

Contact: William J. Haltigan

. . . .

RHODE ISLAND

Department of Health and Human Services, Region I Office
John F. Kennedy Federal Building
Room 2411
Government Center
Boston, MA 02203
(617) 565-1500

Contact: Maureen Osolnik

Department of Labor
Employment and Training Administration, Region I Office
John F. Kennedy Federal Building
Room 1707
Government Center
Boston, MA 02203
(617) 565-3630

Contact: Robert J. Semler

SOUTH CAROLINA

Department of Health and Human Services, Region IV Office
101 Marietta Tower
Suite 1515
Atlanta, GA 30323
(404) 331-2442

Contact: Earl Forsythe

Department of Labor
Employment and Training Administration, Region IV Office
1371 Peachtree Street, NE
Room 400
Atlanta, GA 30367
(404) 347-4411

Contact: Daniel L. Lowry

STATE AND REGIONAL GOVERNMENT GRANTS

· · · · · · · · · · · · · · · · · · ·

SOUTH DAKOTA

Department of Health and Human Services, Region VIII Office
Federal Building
Room 1185
1961 Stout Street
Denver, CO 80294-3538
(303) 844-3372

Contact: Paul Denham

Department of Labor
Employment and Training Administration, Region VIII Office
Federal Building
Room 1640
1961 Stout Street
Denver, CO 80294
(303) 844-4477

Contact: Luis Sepulveda

Aberdeen Area Indian Health Service
Federal Building
115 - 4th Avenue, SE
Aberdeen, SD 57401
(605) 226-7581

Program: Indian Health Service — Health Management Development Program (Federal program 93.228)

Description: Funding for American Indian projects designed to provide a full range of curative, preventive and rehabilitative health services. Assistance to federally-recognized tribes and tribal organizations. Designed to increase the capability of American Indians to manage their own health programs.
Restrictions: Only federally-recognized tribes and tribal organizations may apply
$ Given: Range of $6,250 - $6.3 million per project; average award is $62,693 (national figures)
Number of Awards: Approximately 100 awards made annually nationwide
Application Information: Contact local Health Service office for standard application forms
Deadline: Submit application 90 days prior to proposed project start date
National Contacts: Kay Carpentier, grants management contact, (301) 443-5204; or B. Bowman, program contact, (301) 443-6840
Local Contact: Terrence Sloan, MD

STATE AND REGIONAL GOVERNMENT GRANTS

· ·

TENNESSEE

Department of Health and Human Services, Region IV Office
101 Marietta Tower
Suite 1515
Atlanta, GA 30323
(404) 331-2442

Contact: Earl Forsythe

Department of Labor
Employment and Training Administration, Region IV Office
1371 Peachtree Street, NE
Room 400
Atlanta, GA 30367
(404) 347-4411

Contact: Daniel L. Lowry

Nashville Area Indian Health Service
3310 Perimeter Hill Drive
Nashville, TN 37211
(615) 736-5104

Program: Indian Health Service — Health Management Development Program (Federal program 93.228)
Description: Funding for American Indian projects designed to provide a full range of curative, preventive and rehabilitative health services. Assistance to federally-recognized tribes and tribal organizations. Designed to increase the capability of American Indians to manage their own health programs.
Restrictions: Only federally-recognized tribes and tribal organizations may apply
$ Given: Range of $6,250 - $6.3 million per project; average award is $62,693 (national figures)
Number of Awards: Approximately 100 awards made annually nationwide
Application Information: Contact local Health Service office for standard application forms
Deadline: Submit application 90 days prior to proposed project start date
National Contacts: Kay Carpentier, grants management contact, (301) 443-5204; or B. Bowman, program contact, (301) 443-6840
Local Contact: James Meredith

STATE AND REGIONAL GOVERNMENT GRANTS

. . . .

TEXAS

Department of Health and Human Services, Region VI Office
1200 Main Tower Building
Room 1100
Dallas, TX 75202
(214) 767-3301

Contact: J.B. Keith

Department of Labor
Employment and Training Administration, Region VI Office
525 Griffin Street
Room 317
Dallas, TX 75202
(214) 767-8263

Contact: Floyd E. Edwards

UTAH

Department of Health and Human Services, Region VIII Office
Federal Building
Room 1185
1961 Stout Street
Denver, CO 80294-3538
(303) 844-3372

Contact: Paul Denham

Department of Labor
Employment and Training Administration, Region VIII Office
Federal Building
Room 1640
1961 Stout Street
Denver, CO 80294
(303) 844-4477

Contact: Luis Sepulveda

STATE AND REGIONAL GOVERNMENT GRANTS

. . . .

VERMONT

Department of Health and Human Services, Region I Office
John F. Kennedy Federal Building
Room 2411
Government Center
Boston, MA 02203
(617) 565-1500

Contact: Maureen Osolnik

Department of Labor
Employment and Training Administration, Region I Office
John F. Kennedy Federal Building
Room 1707
Government Center
Boston, MA 02203
(617) 565-3630

Contact: Robert J. Semler

VIRGINIA

Department of Health and Human Services, Region III Office
3535 Market Street
Room 11480
Gateway Building
Philadelphia, PA 19104
MAIL ADDRESS: P.O. Box 13716, Mail Stop No. 1, Philadelphia, PA 19101
(215) 596-6492

Contact: James Mengel

Department of Labor
Employment and Training Administration, Region III Office
P.O. Box 8796
Philadelphia, PA 19101
(215) 596-6336

Contact: William J. Haltigan

STATE AND REGIONAL GOVERNMENT GRANTS

. . . .

WASHINGTON

Department of Health and Human Services, Region X Office
2201 Sixth Avenue
RX-01
Seattle, WA 98121
(206) 553-0420

Contact: Elizabeth G. Healy

Department of Labor
Employment and Training Administration, Region X Office
Federal Office Building
909 First Avenue
Room 1136
Seattle, WA 98174
(206) 442-7700

Contact: Armando Quriz

WEST VIRGINIA

Department of Health and Human Services, Region III Office
3535 Market Street
Room 11480
Gateway Building
Philadelphia, PA 19104
MAIL ADDRESS: P.O. Box 13716, Mail Stop No. 1, Philadelphia, PA 19101
(215) 596-6492

Contact: James Mengel

Department of Labor
Employment and Training Administration, Region III Office
P.O. Box 8796
Philadelphia, PA 19101
(215) 596-6336

Contact: William J. Haltigan

WISCONSIN

Department of Health and Human Services, Region V Office
105 West Adams
23rd Floor
Chicago, IL 60603
(312) 353-5132

Contact: Hiroshi Kanno

Department of Labor
Employment and Training Administration, Region V Office
230 S. Dearborn Street
Room 628
Chicago, IL 60604
(312) 353-0313

Contact: Joseph Juarez

WYOMING

Department of Health and Human Services, Region VIII Office
Federal Building
Room 1185
1961 Stout Street
Denver, CO 80294-3538
(303) 844-3372

Contact: Paul Denham

Department of Labor
Employment and Training Administration, Region VIII Office
Federal Building
Room 1640
1961 Stout Street
Denver, CO 80294
(303) 844-4477

Contact: Luis Sepulveda

STATE AND REGIONAL GOVERNMENT GRANTS

• • • • • • • • • • • • • • • • • • •

PUERTO RICO

Department of Health and Human Services, Region II Office
26 Federal Plaza
Room 3835
New York, NY 10278
(212) 264-4600

Contact: Kathleen Harten

Department of Labor
Employment and Training Administration, Region II Office
201 Varick Steet
Room 755
New York, NY 10014
(212) 337-2139

Contact: Thomas E. Hill

VIRGIN ISLANDS

Department of Health and Human Services, Region II Office
26 Federal Plaza
Room 3835
New York, NY 10278
(212) 264-4600

Contact: Kathleen Harten

Department of Labor
Employment and Training Administration, Region II Office
201 Varick Steet
Room 755
New York, NY 10014
(212) 337-2139

Contact: Thomas E. Hill

Federal Grants

The following chapter includes a limited number of health-related financial assistance programs funded by the federal government. Some of these listings (Community Health Centers, Migrant and Seasonal Farmworker Programs, and Migrant Health Centers Grants) are detailed descriptions of federal programs administered through the regional offices listed in the previous chapter. If one of these programs seems appropriate for your funding needs, please refer back to the previous chapter, "State and Regional Government Grants," for the address of the Department of Health and Human Services office or the Department of Labor office serving your state.

Other listings in this chapter include Medicare programs, funding for health services in rural communities, and several programs for U.S. veterans. If you fall into one of these funding categories, this chapter may direct you to good funding possibilities.

Remember, federal grant sources are not as narrowly defined in purpose or as accessible to individuals as private sector funders. Often, however, the dollar amounts are larger and worth the trouble.

Before you call the contact person for any agency, I suggest that you make a list of what it is you need monies for (i.e., hospital bills, long-term care costs, loss of income replacement). Ask yourself such questions as, are there demonstrated financial needs on the part of the patient or the patient's family? In this fashion, you can address every issue leading to support and aid in one telephone call — by being able to describe precisely the kinds of funding for which you may be eligible.

When you call, ask this: "What types of funding programs do you provide?" If the response does not include a program that meets your particular needs, ask more specific questions. If the agency you call does not offer a program to meet your needs, someone there may be able to direct you to an agency that does. If the agency publishes materials describing its funding programs, request that these be mailed to you, along with an application. Also make sure to find out if there is a deadline coming up, so that you will be able to return any applications by that time.

COMMUNITY HEALTH CENTERS

PROGRAM HEADQUARTERS
Division Primary Care Services,
Bureau of Health Care Delivery and Assistance,
Health Resources and Services Administration,
Public Health Service,
Department of Health and Human Services,
Room 7A-55
Parklawn Building
5600 Fishers Lane
Rockville, MD 20857
(301) 443-2260
Contact: Richard Bohrer, Director

and

GRANTS MANAGEMENT
Bureau of Health Care Delivery and Assistance,
Health Resources and Services Administration,
Public Health Service,
Department of Health and Human Services,
12100 Parklawn Drive
Rockville, MD 20857
(301) 443-5902
Contact: Gary Houseknecht, Grants Management Officer

Program: Community Health Centers (Federal program 93.224)

Description: Project grants to support the development and operation of community health centers that provide primary and supplemental health services to medically-underserved populations. Priority on improving availability, accessibility and organization within these communities. Funds may be used for buying or modernizing buildings, as well as for acquiring special purpose equipment.

Restrictions: Public and nonprofit private agencies, institutions and organizations, plus a limited number of State and local governments, may apply

$ Given: Range of $25,000 - $4 million per award; average award is $1.2 million (national figures)

Application Information: Forms may be obtained from regional offices of the Department of Health and Human Services **(see previous chapter)**

FEDERAL GRANTS

. . . .

MEDICARE — HOSPITAL INSURANCE

Bureau of Program Operations
Room 300
Meadows East Building
Health Care Financing
Administration
Baltimore, MD 21207
(301) 966-5874

Program: Medicare — Hospital Insurance (Federal program 93.773)

Description: Hospital insurance protection for covered services to persons age 65 or above, as well as to certain disabled persons and individuals with chronic renal disease. Benefits paid to participating and emergency hospitals, skilled nursing facilities, home health agencies, and hospice agencies to cover reasonable cost of medically necessary services.

Restrictions: Persons age 65 and over, as well as certain disabled persons and individuals with chronic renal disease, are eligible. A person reaching age 65 after 1968 may need some work credit to qualify for hospital insurance benefits.

$ Given: Based on reasonable costs of necessary services; deductibles and co-insurance payments may be required

Application Information: Call or visit your local Social Security office; persons entitled to Social Security are enrolled automatically, without application

Contact: Local Social Security office (check telephone listings); national headquarters contact, Barbara Gagel, Director, Bureau of Program Operations

. . . .

MEDICARE — SUPPLEMENTARY MEDICAL INSURANCE

Bureau of Program Operations
Room 300
Meadows East Building
Health Care Financing
Administration
Baltimore, MD 21207
(301) 966-5874

Program: Medicare — Supplemental Medical Insurance (Federal program 93.774)

Description: Elective medical insurance coverage for persons age 65 or over, for certain disabled persons, and for individuals with chronic renal disease. Benefits paid for reasonable charges for covered medical services.

Restrictions: All persons age 65 and over, and those under 65 who are eligible for Medicare Hospital Insurance, are eligible; enrollment is voluntary

$ Given: Individual responsible for annual $100 deductible. Thereafter, Medicare pays 80% of reasonable costs for covered services. Monthly premium is assessed; current base premium is $29.90. Some states pay the monthly premium on behalf of qualifying individuals.

Application Information: Call or visit your local Social Security office. Persons entitled to Medicare Hospital Insurance may be enrolled automatically in this program. Coverage may be declined.

Deadline: General enrollment period is the first three months of each year. If coverage is declined initially, it can be accepted later with increased monthly premiums. Special enrollment periods may be available.

Contact: Local Social Security office (check telephone listings); national headquarters contact, Barbara Gagel, Director, Bureau of Program Operations

FEDERAL GRANTS

. . . .

MIGRANT AND SEASONAL FARMWORKER PROGRAMS

**Office of Special
Targeted Programs**
Division of Seasonal
Farmworker Programs
Employment and Training
Administration
Department of Labor
Room N-4641
200 Constitution Avenue,
NW
Washington, DC 20210
(202) 535-0500

Program: Migrant and Seasonal Farmworker Programs
(Federal program 17.247)
Description: Supportive services for individuals who
suffer chronic seasonal unemployment and underemploy-
ment in the agricultural industry. Farmworkers and their
dependents may be offered supportive services, including
health services, to enable them to obtain or retain
employment.
Restrictions: Public and governmental agencies, as well
as private nonprofit organizations authorized by their
charters to operate employment and training programs,
are eligible for funding. Individuals receive services.
$ Given: Approximately $60 - $70 million is allotted on
a national level per program year
Application Information: Individuals should contact their
local Department of Labor, Employment and Training
Administration for details about local service providers
(see previous chapter)
National Contact: Paul Mayrand

• • • • • • • • • • • • • • • • • • •

MIGRANT HEALTH CENTERS GRANTS

PROGRAM HEADQUARTERS
Migrant Health Program
Bureau of Health Care
Delivery and Assistance
Health Resources and
Services Administration
Public Health Service
Department of Health and
Human Services
Room 7A-55
5600 Fishers Lane
Rockville, MD 20857
(301) 443-1153
Contact: Jack Egan, Acting
Director

and

GRANTS MANAGEMENT
Bureau of Health Care
Delivery and Assistance
Health Resources and
Services Administration
Public Health Service
Department of Health and
Human Services
12100 Parklawn Drive
Rockville, MD 20857
(301) 443-5902
Contact: Gary Houseknecht,
Grants Management Officer

Program: Migrant Health Centers Grants (Federal program 93.246)

Description: Funding to support the development and operation of migrant health centers and projects providing primary and supplemental health care services that are accessible to migrant and seasonal agricultural farm workers and their families as they move and work.

Restrictions: Any public or nonprofit private entity may apply. Priority is given to applications from community-based organizations representative of the populations to be served.

$ Given: Range of $30,000 - $1.3 million per project; average award is $300,000

Number of Awards: In FY90, 105 centers served 600,000 migrant/seasonal farm workers

Application Information: Varies by region; contact regional office of the Department of Health and Human Services for details **(see previous chapter)**

FEDERAL GRANTS

• • • • • • • • • • • • • • • • • • •

PREVENTIVE HEALTH AND HEALTH SERVICES BLOCK GRANT

PROGRAM HEADQUARTERS

Center for Chronic Disease Prevention and Health Promotion,
Centers for Disease Control,
Public Health Service,
Department of Health and Human Services,
1600 Clifton Road, NE
Atlanta, GA 30333
(404) 488-5299
Contact: C. Joseph Webb

and

GRANTS MANAGEMENT

Grants Management Branch,
Procurement and Grants Office,
Centers for Disease Control,
Public Health Service,
Department of Health and Human Services,
255 E. Paces Ferry Road, NE
Atlanta, GA 30303
(404) 842-6517
Contact: Harvey Rowe, Grants Management Officer

Program: Preventive Health and Health Services Block Grant (Federal program 93.991)

Description: Funding for preventive health services, including but not limited to: hypertension programs, health incentive activities, health education and risk reduction programs, serum cholesterol control, and uterine and breast cancer services. Programs may include such services as: screening, detection, diagnosis, referral, and follow-up on compliance with prescribed treatments.

Restrictions: Grants are intended primarily for State governments; however, in certain cases, tribes or tribal organizations within the States are eligible. (Two Indian tribes received grant funds in FY90.)

$ Given: Based on a formula, which is based on FY81 State allocations. Recent range of $18,838 - $6 million per award; average award is $1.4 million (national figures)

Application Information: States and tribes may submit applications directly to the national funding agency. No specific format or forms are required. Individuals should inquire about eligibility for program participation at State level, Department of Health and Human Services (see previous chapter).

RURAL HEALTH SERVICES OUTREACH

PROGRAM HEADQUARTERS
Office of Rural Health Policy,
Health Resources and Services Administration,
Public Health Service,
Room 14-22
Parklawn Building
5600 Fishers Lane
Rockville, MD 20857
(301) 443-0835
Contact: Jake Culp,
Associate Administrator

and

GRANTS MANAGEMENT
Grants Management Branch,
Bureau of Health Care Delivery and Assistance,
Health Resources and Services Administration,
Public Health Service,
12100 Parklawn Building
Rockville, MD 20857
(301) 443-5902
Contact: Gary Houseknecht,
Grants Management Officer

Program: Rural Health Services Outreach (Federal program 93.912)
Description: Project grants to allow for provision of medical services to rural populations that are not receiving them. To enhance service capacity or to expand service area; to increase the depth and scope of health services in rural areas
Restrictions: Not-for-profit, public or private entities located in a non-Metropolitan Statistical Area may apply
$ Given: Range of $50,000 - $300,000 per grant; average grant, $200,000
Number of Awards: At least 60 awards were planned for FY91
Application Information: Program guidelines may be obtained from Program Headquarters; write or call the Grants Management Officer for application kit
Deadline: Contact Program Headquarters for deadline dates

FEDERAL GRANTS

. . . .

VETERANS HOSPITALIZATION

Director, Administrative Services
Department of Veterans Affairs
Washington, DC 20420
(202) 535-7384

Program: Veterans Hospitalization (Federal program 64.009)

Description: Provides inpatient medical, surgical and neuropsychiatric care and related medical and dental services to eligible veterans.

Restrictions: Benefits available to any veteran who (1) requires treatment for a service-connected disability or disease, or (2) has a service-connected disability but is in need of treatment for a nonservice-connected condition, or (3) has been honorably discharged and meets minimum active duty requirements, or (4) receives a VA pension, or is a former POW. Benefits are also available to the spouse or child of a veteran with total, permanent disability resulting from a service-connected disability, as well as to the widow, widower or child of a veteran who died as a result of such disability, and to the surviving spouse or child of a person who died on active duty. Medicare and CHAMPUS eligibility may interfere with VA benefits. Nonservice disabled veterans with incomes above certain levels may be treated on a resource-available basis and must agree to pay applicable co-payments.

$ Given: Services provided; approximately $7.5 billion is allotted annually nationwide for services provided through this program

Application Information: Eligible persons may apply personally at a VA Medical Center, through any veterans service organization representative, or by mailing VA Form 10-10 to the nearest VA health care facility

Contact: Local VA Medical Center

. . . .

VETERANS HOSPITAL BASED HOME CARE

Assistant Chief Medical Director for Geriatrics and Extended Care
Department of Veterans Affairs
Washington, DC 20420
(202) 535-7530

Program: Veterans Hospital Based Home Care (Federal program 64.022)
Description: Provides individual medical, nursing, social, and rehabilitative services to eligible veterans in their home environment by VA hospital staff. Provided as follow-up to inpatient status at VA facility only.
Restrictions: Benefits available to veterans requiring intermittent skilled nursing care and related medical services for a protracted period of time. Individuals must meet criteria for VA Hospitalization (Federal program 64.009). Medical determination as to need for home health services is made by a VA hospital physician.
$ Given: Services provided; approximately $30 million allotted annually for this program, nationwide
Contact: Hospital Based Home Care Program Coordinator, or local Veterans Administration

VETERANS NURSING HOME CARE

Assistant Chief Medical Director for Geriatrics and Extended Care
Department of Veterans Affairs
Washington, DC 20420
(202) 535-7179

Program: Veterans Nursing Home Care (Federal program 64.010)
Description: Services for eligible veterans who are not acutely ill and not in need of hospital care, but who require skilled nursing care, related medical services, supportive personal care, and individual adjustment services in a homelike atmosphere.
Restrictions: Veterans must require skilled nursing care and related medical services for a protracted period of time. Individuals must meet criteria for VA Hospitalization (Federal program 64.009). Medical determination as to need for nursing home care is made by a VA hospital physician.
$ Given: Nursing home care services provided; approximately $660-$840 million allotted annually nationwide for this program
Contact: VA Nursing Home Care Program Coordinator, or local Veterans Administration

FEDERAL GRANTS

• •

VETERANS OUTPATIENT CARE

**Director, Administrative
Services**
Department of Veterans
Affairs
Washington, DC 20420
(202) 535-7384

Program: Veterans Outpatient Care (Federal program 64.011)
Description: Provides medical and dental services, medicines, and medical supplies to eligible veterans on an outpatient basis. Includes: examination, treatment, some home health services, podiatric, optometric, dental, supportive medical services and surgical services. Readjustment counseling for Vietnam era veterans. Drugs, medicines, prosthetic appliances, transportation, and other reasonable and necessary supplies also provided.
Restrictions: Eligibility requirements are similar but not identical to those for Veterans Hospitalization (Federal program 64.009). Check with local Veterans Administration for details.
$ Given: Services and goods provided; approximately $3 - $3.5 billion is allotted annually nationwide for this program
Contact: Local VA Medical Center

VETERANS PRESCRIPTION SERVICE

**Assistant Chief Medical
Director for Clinical
Affairs**
Department of Veterans
Affairs
Washington, DC 20420
(202) 233-3277

Program: Veterans Prescription Service (Federal program 64.012)
Description: Provides eligible veterans and certain dependents and survivors with prescription drugs and expendable prosthetic medical supplies from VA pharmacies upon presentation of prescription(s) from a licensed physician. Prescriptions must be as specific therapy in treatment of illness or injury suffered by veteran; dispensed by VA pharmacists directly to veterans or dispatched through the mail. Refill service available on physician's authorization. Where there are no VA pharmacies, payment for prescribed drugs is reimbursed. Co-payment may be required from veterans with prescriptions for nonservice-related conditions.
Restrictions: Open to veterans in treatment for service-connected conditions or for conditions that required hospitalization and now require continued care on an outpatient basis. Other veterans may also be eligible.
Contact: Local VA Medical Center

Index

209

COMPANIES/CORPORATIONS

Books in Laurie Blum's **Free Money** Series

•   •   •   •   •   •   •   •   •   •   •   •   •   •   •   •   •   •   •

THE FREE MONEY FOR CHILD CARE SERIES

Free Money for Day Care
• Advice on finding financial aid for family day care, child care centers, in-house care, and camp and summer programs

Free Money for Private Schools
• Where to find money for preschool and nursery education, private primary schools, and private secondary schools

Free Money for Children's Medical and Dental Care
• Ways to receive money for both long- and short-term medical care, dental and orthodontic treatment, and dermatological procedures

Free Money for Behavioral and Genetic Childhood Disorders
• Free Money for treatment of learning disabilities, eating disorders, retardation, alcohol and drug abuse, neurological disturbances, and sleep disorders

THE FREE MONEY FOR HEALTH CARE SERIES

Free Money for Diseases of Aging
• Find money to help pay for major surgery and medical care for diseases of aging such as Alzheimer's, Parkinson's, stroke, and other chronic illnesses

Free Money for Heart Disease and Cancer Care
• Ways to receive money for the diagnosis and treatment (surgery or long-term care) of cancer and heart disease

Free Money for Fertility Treatments
• Where to look for Free Money for infertility testing, treatment, insemination, and preliminary adoption expenses

Free Money for the Care and Treatment of Mental and Emotional Disorders
• Detailed guidance on locating Free Money for psychological care